MW00461464

YOU GOTTA LET
God Finish!

SIOHVAUGHN FUNCHES

©2018 Siohvaughn Funches. All rights reserved. No part of this publication may be reproduced, distributed, or transmitted in any form or by any means, including photocopying, recording, or other electronic or mechanical methods, without the prior written permission of the author, except in the case of brief quotations embodied in critical reviews and certain other noncommercial uses permitted by copyright law.

ISBN: 978-1-54394-316-0

SPECIAL DEDICATIONS

My Lord and Savior

I especially dedicate this book to my Lord and Savior, Jesus Christ. Without You Lord, I can do nothing, but through You, the most amazing things have happened! You have poured out Your Spirit upon me, in order for me to pour out Your Spirit upon Your people through this book. My prayer is that Your purpose will be accomplished through this masterwork of Your own hands and heart, and Your people will never be the same for Your glory and for their good, in Your name Jesus, I pray

My Family

I also want to dedicate this book to my loving family. Mama, I appreciate who you are and all you have done. I'm honored to have you as a mother. Granny, I love you and thank you for the way you love me…unconditionally. To my sons, who I love more than all the sand by all the seas, and more than all the leaves on all the trees, you all are gifts sent from God. May Jesus always bless and keep you, cause His face to shine upon you, lift up His countenance upon you and grant to you His shalom beyond measure in Jesus name I pray.

CONTENTS

INTRODUCTION

All the promises of God in Christ are yes, and in Him amen...
(2 Corinthians. 1:20)

The Lord let me know the primary reason He wrote this book through me is because of His love for His people. God has seen you giving up, fearing, and losing hope concerning His promises for your life, and He has come through me to restore to some, and reveal to others, a very powerful truth that will cause you to rise above the negative and receive all He has for you. In order to do that, God wants us to see through the Word of God into the very the heart of Jesus, because therein is found all we need in order to receive all God has for us. Abba, your heavenly Father, reveals Jesus, and His heart of love for you in this book, by looking more deeply at the scriptures through the lives of His people in His Word, my own life and the life of Jesus. God has ordained it that His Son Jesus, His unfailing love for us, and His flawless ways are all revealed through the lives of God's children. The entire bible is proof of that truth. Throughout it, God is revealing His Son, His love and His ways to us. By way of example, in the beginning of the Bible, God created Adam, the first man, who was a type of Jesus (Romans 5:14). At the end of the Bible, the book of Revelation opens up stating, "The revelation of Jesus Christ, which God gave Him to show His servants..." (Revelation 1:1). Again, throughout the entire Bible, God is revealing Jesus, and God wants to do the same thing today through this book, because, by doing so, God will set you free from all attacks from hopelessness, fear, depression, rejection, discouragement, and every negative evil that has come against you, and you will receive all He has for you. We see herein how God does this time and time again for His people, regardless of the opposition. And, the good news is this; "God is not a respecter of persons," what He has done for others, He is willing and able to do for you (Acts 10:34 & Romans 2:11). Not only that, but as you behold Jesus, the Holy Spirit transforms you into His very same image (2 Corinthians 3:18). (This is what I call effortless transformation!) And as we journey together through this book with the Lord on our own personal "road to Emmaus" experience, like those who Jesus taught when He first rose from the dead, we too, will go from feelings of despair and hopelessness to eye-opening deliverance, joy, understanding, and powerful breakthroughs that will be remembered for generations (Luke 24:13-35). We too will know without any doubt that the Lord loves us deeply and He has not forgotten us, or any of the promises He made us, and neither has He forgotten the desires He placed in our hearts. Therefore, let us not lose heart, or give up, especially those of us who have waited for many years to receive from God the miracles we long for, because God has not forgotten us either, and He has not changed His mind. God understands that for some of us who have waited years for God to manifest the miracle we desire, that "the wait" has become "a weight" and thus, God has come to deliver you from that heaviness and restore faith, hope and strength in you, so you can receive the promises of God and see every miracle you desire manifest! All you have to do is what God taught me while I was on the brink of giving up; "You gotta let God finish!" The strength and ability to do so is found in looking at the heart of Jesus through the lives of His people.

It was this revelation that God gave me that literally kept me from despairing and positioned me to receive promise after promise from Him. Needless to say, every area of my life has been transformed for the better and because God is such a big giver and loves you too, He birthed this powerful book through me and commissioned me to share this revelation with you so that every area of your life will also be transformed for the better!

God is faithful even if we are faithless... (2 Timothy 2:13)

CHAPTER 1:

THE LORD IS WITH YOU!

You will not need to fight in this battle. Position yourselves,
stand still and see the salvation of the Lord,
who is with you. (2 Chronicles 20:17).

ONE DAY WHILE SPENDING TIME WITH GOD, I TOLD HIM I
wanted to know what does it mean, "The Lord is with you." I was
going through a very trying time, and I told God bluntly, "I keep
hearing people say and the Bible says, 'The Lord is with you,' but I
don't need somebody to be with me as another spectator looking on
my affliction. I need help!"

God was very gracious to me, and didn't rebuke me at all for
my straightforwardness or my tone. Instead He took me to the life
story of Joseph in the Bible and taught me what it means to have the
Lord with you. My life hasn't been the same since and all for the better. I'm so glad that I prayed to God for this understanding, because
when God answers prayers…He answers them well beyond what we
asked Him for. Thus, when God answered me, He didn't just give me

the understanding I desired, He also opened my eyes to see Jesus hidden in the life of Joseph. And God let me know that He didn't just reveal these life-changing truths for my sake, but so that I can share them with you as well. Our God is very good and gracious! So let's go together now on this life journey of Joseph's, and receive the understanding God is giving us about what it means to have the Lord with us…and have our lives transformed for our good and the good of many others!

To Whom Much Is Given, Much Is Required

The Bible opens up the life of Joseph, the son of Jacob, and tells us immediately that Joseph's father loved him more than the rest of his siblings, because Joseph was the child of his father's old age (Genesis 37:3). And Jacob expressed this favor he had for Joseph by making him a tunic distinctive in colors and having long sleeves (which many Bible translations call a coat of many colors). Perhaps not surprisingly to some reading this, Joseph's older brothers hated him because they saw that their father loved him more than them (Genesis 37:4). Thus, the drama began.

One night, God gave Joseph a dream, which he shared with his brothers. In the dream all of the brothers, including Joseph, were binding sheaves and behold, Joseph's sheaves arose and stood upright, but his brother's sheaves all bowed down to his sheaf (Genesis 37:7). When Joseph shared this dream with his brothers, the Bible tells us that they hated him even more than before. Then God gave Joseph another dream. In this second dream, the sun, the moon, and eleven stars bowed down to him. Joseph again shared this dream with his brothers…and also his parents. The result…his father rebuked him, but kept the dream in mind and his brothers envied him all the more! There is no question that these dreams both came from God, and they are dreams of destiny and purpose for Joseph. However, God taught me from looking at the life of Joseph that his decision to tell his brothers the dreams that God gave him, wasn't exactly the best decision given the condition of their hearts toward Joseph. It was not Joseph's responsibility to make his brothers love him instead of hate him, but Joseph had been given much by God, when given those dreams, and to whomever much is given much is required. Usually, this "much" that is required includes seeking God and His will for what to say, whom to say it to and when to say it. In other words, it requires the wisdom and prudence of God. At that time, Joseph lacked prudence and wisdom, but God would use even this lack of understanding and the things Joseph went through, to impart an abundance of wisdom and prudence to him in order to equip him to fulfill his God-given destiny.

We can all learn something valuable from this lesson in Joseph's life…especially those to whom the Lord has committed much. Before unveiling the plans God has for us, we need to seek God and ask Him if they should be revealed, and if so, to whom and in what time.

There is a reason God gave these dreams to Joseph and not anyone else in his family! Not everyone will celebrate the greatness God has for you…and in fact, some won't even tolerate it, doing whatever they can to kill that dream while it is still inside of you. Sadly, family is no exception. Jesus said it best, "A prophet is not without honor except in his own country, among his own relatives, and in his own house" (Mark 6:4). Therefore, we have to walk in the wisdom and prudence of God, even with our own family. This may require more time with God and more praying than others but God told us, to whomever much is given, much is required (Luke 12:48).

Trust The Journey

If there is one powerful lesson I have learned from God looking at the life of Joseph, it is that you can trust the journey God takes you on, because God is indeed faithful (2 Timothy 2:13). God will do for you whatever He promised He would do! Yet, while God is indeed faithful, to us human beings His ways can seem a bit unorthodox at times. The destination (the promise of God) will often make sense to us, but the way God takes us in order to get us to that promised destination could often be unnerving for some of us, and therefore requires our trust in God. We often go through challenging things before reaching the destination, which seem to be less like a detour, and more like a derailment...but God! In moments like that, it is vital to go and turn to the scriptures and meditate on God, and His prosperous ways, especially through the life of Joseph. I say that because the life of Joseph seems to be a clear picture of God promising a destination, while permitting a route to get there that nobody would expect.

Shortly after Joseph shared the dream that God placed in his heart regarding his destiny, his hate-filled brothers plotted his death, having let their unresolved jealously and envy get the better of them (Genesis 37:24). They lay in wait for Joseph to come near to them in a field away from their home in order to kill him, but because God had a plan for Joseph's life, as much as they wanted him dead, they could not carry out their wicked plan. Instead they cast Joseph into a pit, and later sold him as a slave to some Ishmaelite slave-traders. Afterward, the Bible says, "...Joseph had been taken down to Egypt. And Potiphar, an officer of Pharaoh, captain of the guard, an Egyptian, bought him from the Ishmaelite's who had taken him down there" (Genesis 39:1). Now, if you place yourself in Joseph's shoes at that point, and look at your life in that moment, it would likely seem absolutely crazy! Joseph just went from dreaming about being in a God-given position of leadership, to being betrayed by his own brothers and sold as an Egyptian slave! In other words, Joseph was promised the mountaintop, and not long afterwards, was taken by force to what appears to be rock bottom.

Let's be honest, people: Lesser things have led to full-blown anxiety and depression! Joseph has seemingly lost everything. His family is gone, his dignity has departed, and he has no money, no freedom, and no ability to get himself out of this mess. All of his material possessions are gone; he literally has nothing monetary or material. This is much like a barren womb in many regards. Not only is it empty, it is also devoid of a way to produce something. Many of us can probably relate to Joseph in this moment, because we have experienced a time of seeming bareness. But I thank God, because He is an expert at bringing something out of absolutely nothing! Remember, God is Elohim, the Creator. In the beginning, "[t]he earth was without form and *void...*" (Genesis 1:2). Yet God just spoke, and the earth as we know it was formed and filled (Genesis 1:3-24). This is why our powerful God tells us whenever we are facing a barren situation, to rejoice and prepare our lives to be filled (Isaiah 54:1-3). God is telling His children in Isaiah 54 that we can rejoice and prepare to bear fruit despite any barren circumstance! Our God tells us this because He is the same yesterday, today, and forevermore (Hebrew 13:8). Therefore, the same God who in the beginning spoke to an empty earth and filled it with a Word, is the same God, who can speak to any emptiness in your life and with a Word, bring fullness out of it, that you don't even have room enough to receive (Malachi 3:10). Thus, "fear not little flock, it is your Father's good pleasure to give you the Kingdom" (Luke 12:32).

Now, albeit, Joseph didn't have anything you could see with the eye but his life, the Bible tells us the one thing that Joseph did have is this: "**The Lord was with Joseph**, and he was a successful man... And his master saw that **the Lord was with him** and that the Lord made all he did prosper in his hand. So Joseph found favor in his sight, and served him...So it was, from the time that he had made him overseer of his house and all that he had, that the Lord blessed the Egyptian's house for Joseph's sake; and the blessing of the Lord was on all that he had in the house and in the field" (Genesis 39:2-6). We can see right away that the Lord being with Joseph caused him to be successful and gave him favor with the ruler of that time. Now, before this chapter concludes, God will reveal to us even the more, the power of having the Lord with us, even if we don't have anything, or anyone else…and any of you who thought you had nothing, will realize you have everything because the Lord is with you!

Now, some time after Joseph was promoted to overseer of his master's house, things in his life took another drastic turn…for what surely seems like the worse. The Bible says, Joseph was handsome in form and appearance. And it came to pass that his master's wife cast longing eyes on Joseph, and she said, "Lie with me." But he refused and said to his master's wife, "Look my master does not know what is with me in the house, and he has committed all that he has to my hand…How then can I do this great wickedness, and sin against God?" (Genesis 39:6-9). Well, I wish I could tell you that this denied damsel changed her mind and realized it is wrong to have an affair with her husband's worker; but she didn't. Instead, she became furious at Joseph and falsely accused him of raping her (Genesis 39:11-19). And as to be expected, Joseph's master was angry. Then he had Joseph sent to prison…for a crime he didn't commit (Genesis 39:20). Going from bad to worse is an understatement. Joseph was already a slave, which is rock bottom. Then he was falsely accused of raping a ruler's wife and falsely imprisoned, which is below rock bottom! He was doubly confined at this point. As a slave he wasn't free, but as an imprisoned slave the confinement and loss of freedom was double. But despite this seeming hardship, the Bible says, "the Lord was with Joseph and showed him mercy, and He gave him favor in the sight of the keeper of the prison. And [t]he keeper committed to Joseph's hand all the prisoners who were in the prison…." The keeper of the prison did not look into anything that was under Joseph's authority, because the Lord was with him; and whatever he did, the Lord made it prosper" (Genesis 39:23). We can see right here that the blessing of God followed Joseph wherever he went because the blessing was upon him. When Joseph was with his daddy, he was highly favored. When they sold him into slavery, he was highly favored and when they put him in prison, favor followed him in! This teaches us that when the Lord is with you, the blessings of the Lord are too…wherever you go! That is one of the powerful ways of our loving God!

Now, God, who is amazing, also showed me another truth about His ways. He had Joseph in a position of power like a warden of a prison, while simultaneously serving a sentence as a slave! God promotes His children both in the prison, and as we will soon see, while in the palace. This has surely taught me that God is gracious to us while we are on the mountaintop, and He is gracious to us when we are in the valley-low. With God all things are possible (Matthew 19:26). After all, God is the one who declares He makes rivers in the desert (Isaiah 43:19). Someone in the desert would think that they need to come out of the desert in order to have their thirst quenched and to be refreshed, but God is able to bring the rivers to you…even in the desert! This truth is why we can indeed trust the journey God choses in order to take us to our destination. Joseph certainly discovered this truth about God.

One day while Joseph was in prison, both the chief butler and chief baker of the king of Egypt wronged the king, and therefore Pharaoh was angry with them, and had them thrown into prison (Genesis 40:1-3). When they arrived, the captain of the guard charged Joseph with serving them. One night while in jail both the chief butler and the chief baker had a dream, "and each man's dream with its own interpretation" (Genesis 40:5). When they awoke, they both were sad because they both had dreams, but they didn't have anyone to interpret the dreams for them. Joseph, being fully aware of God's presence with Him and His power...even inside the prison, said to them, "Do not interpretations belong to God? Tell them to me, please" (Genesis 40:8). When the chief butler told Joseph his dream, God gave the interpretation and told him that his dream meant that "within three days Pharaoh will lift up your head and restore you to your place, and you will put Pharaoh's cup in his hand according to the former manner" (Genesis 40:13). Once the chief baker heard the interpretation that God gave through Joseph for the butler, he wanted his dream interpreted too. After explaining to Joseph the details of his dream, God provided the interpretation, and Joseph explained to the chief baker, "this is the interpretation of it... within three days Pharaoh will lift off your head from you and hang you on a tree; and the birds will eat your flesh from you" (Genesis 40:18-19). And as sure as God cannot lie, within three days; the chief butler was taken from prison and restored, but the chief baker was hung and died (Genesis 40:21).

Now, Joseph, relying on a human to save him, pleaded with the chief butler that when he is restored to his position as Pharaoh's butler, "remember me when it is well with you, and please show kindness to me; make mention of me to Pharaoh, and get me out of this house" (Genesis 40:14). However, the butler forgot Joseph. Needless to say, Joseph quickly learned a lesson many of us already have: only Jesus saves (Acts 4:12). Now that was likely very difficult for Joseph, but it certainly wasn't the only lesson he had to learn. God had undoubtedly given Joseph dreams concerning himself too, and the interpretation of that dream was divine leadership, yet Joseph had not seen his own dream come to pass...yet he was witnessing God give others dreams, which were made a reality right before his eyes! Joseph indeed had to learn to trust God, because it looked like God remembered others but forgot him. But we know from the life of Joseph and how it concludes that God had not forgotten him at all! This too, is a lesson for us. When we are waiting on God to manifest the promise He made us and it seems to be taking a long time, yet we see others around us having their dreams come to pass, we like Joseph, have to continue to trust in the goodness and faithfulness of God. We must believe the truth; God has not forgotten us!

Just two years later, and all in one day, God gave Pharaoh a dream that troubled him, and prevented everyone on Pharaoh's staff from giving the interpretation of that dream… which Pharaoh so desperately wanted. God caused the Chief Butler to repent for his faults, recall Joseph, and tell of Joseph's ability to interpret dreams. Immediately God made Joseph, a prisoner in a dungeon, known to the most powerful man in Egypt, had him groomed, and brought before the king of an entire nation! God wasn't done. Pharaoh explained to Joseph the two dreams he had, and God gave Joseph the interpretation of them both. Joseph explained to Pharaoh that the two dreams were one in the same and that God was showing Pharaoh something He was about to do. Seven years of plenty were about to come to the land of Egypt; but following that, seven years of famine would hit the land, and the famine would be very severe (Genesis 41:31). Then God gave Joseph the wisdom to prepare for the famine so that the people would not die from hunger: "Collect one-fifth of the produce of the land of Egypt in the seven plentiful years…then that food shall be as a reserve for the land for the seven years of famine which shall be in the land of Egypt, that the land may not perish during the famine" (Genesis 41:34 & 36). Look at God! Taking the same Joseph who lacked wisdom to deal with a few brothers of his, to having such an overflow of wisdom, the answer to save a nation was in him alone!

Still in the same day, Pharaoh said, "Inasmuch as God has shown you all this, there is no one as discerning and wise as you. You shall be over my house, and all my people shall be ruled according to your word; only in regard to the throne will I be greater than you" (Genesis 41:39-40). God then had Pharaoh array Joseph in fine linen, place a gold chain around his neck, and have him ride in the second chariot belonging to Pharaoh, while they cried out "Bow the knee" before Joseph. Then God gave Joseph an Egyptian bride, hand picked by the king of Egypt himself. With this wife, Joseph had two children. The firstborn was named Manasseh, which means "For God has made me forget all my toil and all my father's house." His second son he called, Ephraim, which translates as "For God has caused me to be fruitful in the land of my affliction" (Genesis 41:51-52). God had clearly given Joseph more than what he ever dreamed of having. And what the Lord did for Joseph He will do for you too, because He is with you also!

Needless to say, the seven years of plenty came just as God had promised, and right after that, the seven years of famine hit the land. During the years of plenty, God gave Joseph wisdom, and he "gathered very much grain, as the sand of the sea, until he stopped counting, for it was immeasurable" (Genesis 41:49). During the famine, Joseph opened up the storehouses to provide for the people of Egypt to save them from perishing. The famine was so severe it reached beyond Egypt into the land of Canaan, the place where Joseph came from. God used this to cause Joseph's family to come to Egypt to purchase grain in order to live and not die of starvation. They came for food, but found their long-lost family member reigning over a nation in power and authority, and when they came into Joseph's presence; they bowed before him… thus fulfilling the dream God gave Joseph. And in addition to that, Joseph forgave his brothers, was reunited with his father whom he loved, and saved the lives of his entire family…and an entire nation (Genesis 47).

God is indeed amazing! But let me be the first to say that the journey that God took Joseph on didn't look like it led to the dream that God promised. It looked like one disaster after another, and appeared as though God had forgotten what He promised Joseph. Nothing could have been further from the truth. God was orchestrating events the entire time, and causing everything to work together for Joseph's good. The good news for us? God is the same yesterday, today, and forevermore (Hebrews 13:8). God's ways are the same. This means we don't have to panic even if darkness is all around, because God takes darkness and turns it into the most brilliant and beautiful light! God takes ashes and turns them into beauty, and He takes weeping and turns it into dancing (Isaiah 61:3). This means we can truly fear not, because God is with us, like He was with Joseph, but even greater because we are in Christ Jesus. But albeit this is true there is a journey before the destination and therefore; we have to do what Joseph did: we have to let God finish! We have to trust God's unfailing Word that He who began a good work in us is faithful to finish it (Philippians 1:6). He did it for Joseph, and He is doing it for us. Trust God. He loves you and delights in giving you His best (Luke 12:32).

Your Dream Is Coming To Pass!

Joseph's life is proof that God will do what He promised you, regardless of any opposition! When it came to Joseph's life, we see both hell and high water, so-to-speak, coming against him...but because of the faithfulness of God, all that He promised Joseph He did and much more! It did not look like Joseph's dream was coming to pass, however. In fact it looked like he was getting further and further from the possibility of that happening. Joseph had nothing materially, and he had absolutely no way out of the trouble he was in. Joseph was an imprisoned slave! Joseph was in double bondage in a foreign land, far from friends and forsaken by his own brothers. He had every reason to give up and not believe God, yet we see that Joseph persevered in faith and believed that the Lord was with him...even when it seemed to be going from bad to worse.

We can learn so much from looking at Joseph's life. He was a wise man indeed. He was wise for saving the people from perishing, and most wise for believing in the faithfulness of God, and not giving up on the dreams God gave him. And we are blessed today because he chose to let God finish. As a result, we see through his life a most powerful truth about God: If God gave you a promise, God will most certainly—no matter what happens—fulfill that promise, and bring that dream to pass. God did it for Joseph, and He is doing it for us. God doesn't show partiality with people. What He did for one He is willing and able to do for you. This is an unfailing truth that we can totally rest in!

Now, in addition to the specific promises and dreams God has put in our individual hearts, God has also promised us that all the promises of God in Christ are yes, and in Him amen to the glory of God (2 Corinthians 1:20). The Bible is filled with these promises from God, and because of what Jesus did at the cross, fulfilling the law for us and all of its preconditions to God's promises, we as new covenant believers have a blood-bought right to every one of them! It behooves us therefore to know Jesus and all that He has done for us. Yes, salvation is the most important thing that Jesus provided us, and indeed, Jesus has saved us from hell, death, sin and the consequences of it (Romans 4:25), but Jesus has done so much in addition to this. For example, Jesus became poor so that through His poverty we might become rich (2 Corinthians 8:9). This promise, and all the others in the Bible from God, are ours because of Jesus' sacrifice at the cross and God's unending love for us. We just need to believe…and if you truly believe, you will let God finish…no matter what opposition. God undoubtedly has a good plan for your life, and whatever He has promised you is a part of that plan. And because no plan of God's can be thwarted, the promises God made you likewise cannot be thwarted (Job 42:2).

Also, by looking at the life of Joseph we learn this vital truth about God: Whatever position of appointment God has called you to, God will make sure that your position is secure, and that you are appointed to it. No created thing can stop God from making you who He called you to be, or placing you where He ordained for you to be. This is evinced in the life of Joseph. God ordained for Joseph to be a leader. Nothing could stop this Word of promise from coming to pass. The Bible says that even when Joseph was sold as a slave, he was made overseer of his master's house (Genesis 39:5). Overseer equals leadership. Then Joseph was taken to prison for a crime he didn't commit, but the Bible says that while in prison, Joseph was given charge over the prisoners. "In charge" also equals leadership. Then the grand finale occurred, and Joseph ruled over an entire country, and the Bible says that without his authority nobody could lift up his or her hand or foot in all of Egypt (Genesis. 41:44). That is leadership!

So what have we learned from this? Not betrayal, slavery, false accusations, wrongful convictions, or a life sentence in prison could stop God from making Joseph the leader He called him to be! Therefore, children of God, whatever God says about you, that shall stand…but we, like Joseph, have to let God finish!

Notably, God's calling on Joseph's life to be a leader was manifesting at every stage of his journey to his dream coming to pass. Joseph led as a slave and he led as a prisoner, and albeit Joseph never wanted to be a slave or a prisoner, God was still moving in his life and manifesting who He called him to be during those times. God had a purpose for allowing those times. God used those times in Joseph's life to train Joseph, and prepare him for the ultimate leadership role He had for him over the nation of Egypt. This is why God tells us not to despise small beginnings (Zechariah 4:10). The ways of God are this: When you are faithful over little, God makes you ruler over much (Luke 16:10). Joseph was a faithful leader as a slave. Then he was a faithful leader as a prisoner. Joseph ended up a faithful leader over an entire country!

We also see in the life of Joseph that God doesn't only answer our prayers and bring our dreams to pass; He exceeds our expectations (Ephesians 3:20). Not only did God make Joseph a God-given leader, He blessed him with a bride, and two children, and restored him with his brothers and reunited him with the father whom he loved. In addition to that, God used Joseph to save the life of his entire family and an entire nation. God is good, people! This is how you can know that you know, without any doubts, that God will do everything…and much more, of what He promised you.

Not a created thing can stop God. After all, He is God! Jesus is the Creator of everything seen and unseen. He made the heavens and the earth and everything in it, above it, and beneath it! If you don't know the way, no worries…Jesus said, I am the way. If you need healing, no worries. Jesus is Jehovah Rapha, the Lord your healer (Exodus 15:26). Jesus is everything you could ever need and desire… and more. The Lord said, "I Am that I Am" (Exodus 3:14). God is to you whatever you need Him to be. Whatever the need, God is saying; "I Am!"

To my brothers in sisters in prison, you have to know unequivocally that Jesus can get you out of prison supernaturally. This is true despite what the natural judge has decreed because God is the Judge of all judges, the Lord of all lords and the King of all kings! He is sovereign. Joseph was serving a life sentence in a land where the laws didn't provide for an appeal, but Jesus was with him and Jesus delivered him! Now you, on the other hand, are at least likely to be in a jurisdiction where you can file an appeal. Joseph didn't even have that hope, but he had Jesus, and that was all he needed to be free. Jesus is mindful of you and those held captive are a priority to Jesus. The Lord showed me this one-day while reading Isaiah 61. This is the chapter in the Bible where some of the purpose of Jesus is revealed. The Word says, "The Spirit of the Lord God is upon Me, because the Lord has anointed Me to preach good tidings to the poor; He has sent Me to heal the brokenhearted, to proclaim liberty to the captives, and the opening of the prison to those who are bound" (Isaiah. 61:1). There is something about being bound that Jesus doesn't like for His children, and this is so much so, that while describing His purpose in our lives, He says two times: it is to set us free from bondage! Whenever God speaks it is important, but if He says something more than once…and in this instance back to back…He is emphasizing this truth for a reason! Jesus' will for our lives is that we be free…settle that in your hearts and minds for good. It is the purpose for which Jesus came. To those held captive: Pray boldly to Jesus to be delivered, because freedom is the will of God.

What It Means to Have the Lord with You

As I mentioned earlier, it was during a very trying time for me that I began to ask the Lord to show me what it means to have the Lord with you. I didn't want the Lord to be with me, to look upon my shameful situation, I wanted the Lord to be with me to deliver me. And it was during that time that God explained to me what it meant to have the Lord with you through Joseph's life. So let's expound on it a bit.

Remember that when Joseph was taken captive as a slave, he had nothing outwardly. He had no material possessions, money, friends, or family around. But we can see from looking at his life that the one thing that Joseph did have, was the only thing that Joseph did need: The Lord was with Joseph. And because the Lord was with Joseph, he was successful, favored, and promoted to a position of authority and leadership everywhere he went. This tells us that success, favor, and promotion comes from the Lord, not man, or material gain. And if the Lord is with you, these blessings are with you too.

The Bible also says that because the Lord was with Joseph, the blessings of God were on his master and all that his master had in his house and in his fields (Genesis 39:5). This means that the Lord being with us, blesses not only us, but also those around us! And Joseph's master saw that the Lord was with Joseph and caused all he did to prosper in his hand. This means that others can see that the Lord is with us and that means that the Lord being with us is not just a spiritual blessing, it is also a material blessing that manifests outwardly where others can see it in our lives.

Additionally, having the Lord with us means what it did for Joseph in this regard, too: Whatever Joseph did, the Lord made it prosper! This means prosperity doesn't come from people or human intelligence, prosperity comes from having the Lord with you. This prosperity doesn't just include material possessions or money either. Joseph had a great career, and even greater calling…and his family life was exceedingly blessed.

The Bible also says that having the Lord with you causes the mercy of God to be upon you and His favor to be with you wherever you go. The Lord was with Joseph and showed him mercy, and gave him favor even while in prison (Genesis 39:22). This means that having the Lord with you, even if you are in a dark situation, God turns the darkness it into light. Even if you have been given ashes, the Lord being with you will turn the ashes to beauty. No matter where you are at and what hardship you are facing, if the Lord is with you, His mercy and favor on your life will turn what was meant for evil into good for you!

We also see that having the Lord with Joseph produced such favor from God that while Joseph was in jail for rape, he was put in charge of all the prisoners, and the keeper of the prison didn't bother to look into any of the matters he charged Joseph with. Potiphar's wife tried to ruin Joseph's credibility, but because the Lord was with

Joseph everywhere he went, important people trusted him! When the Lord is with you, people will trust you... and not just any people, but significant people. This trust is also seen when Pharaoh, who just met Joseph for the first time, put him in charge of his entire country and entrusted Joseph with saving the lives of his people...including his very own! It was one thing for Potiphar to trust Joseph with his house and fields. And it was more for the keeper of the prison to trust Joseph with the lives of the prisoners, but it was another level to trust Joseph with the lives of all the people in the whole nation. And all of these blessings are for one reason: The Lord was with Joseph!

Lastly, the Lord showed me in Joseph's life that God made everything work together for Joseph's good; and this too was the result of the Lord being with Joseph. Yes, it was evil for Joseph's brothers to sell him as a slave, but that is what God used to transport Joseph to Egypt, where he later saved the lives of his own family and the lives of an entire nation. And yes, it was wrong for Potiphar's wife to falsely accuse Joseph of rape and make him serve a prison sentence for a crime he didn't commit, but it was in prison that Joseph met and interpreted Pharaoh's butler's dream, who God later used to tell Pharaoh about Joseph when Pharaoh needed his own dream interpreted! That interpretation led to exaltation and Joseph ruled over the land of Egypt second in command only to Pharaoh! It is quite clear in the life of Joseph that when the Lord is with you, all things work together for your good!

In addition to the life of Joseph, God began to expound on the truth of what it means to have the Lord with you through various passages in the Bible. God let me know that having the Lord with you means you do not have to fear evil! By way of example, the Lord showed me Psalm 23:4, which says, "Yea, though I walk through the valley of the shadow of death, I will fear no evil, for You are with me!" He then showed me Psalm 46:1, which says, "God is our refuge and strength, a very present help in trouble. Therefore we will not fear." And God also promises, "the Lord himself goes before you and will be with you; He will never leave you nor forsake you. Do not be afraid; do not be discouraged" (Deuteronomy 31:8). It is evident that when the Lord is with you, you have no reason to fear. Additionally, the Word says, "God is our refuge and strength, a very present help in trouble. Therefore we will not fear" (Psalm 46:1). Notably, God isn't just a present help when it comes to trouble, but He is a **very** present help. God is always with us, but the Holy Spirit is showing us in this Bible verse that if we are in trouble, God is not just a present help; the Lord is **very present to help** us and because of this truth, we have absolutely nothing to fear! It's like God emphasizes His presence, and what it means to have it in our lives when trouble arises. God wants us to rest easy knowing that He is with us, and therefore we don't have anything to fear! Your enemies are the ones who need to shake, rattle, and roll, but not you. The Lord is with you, and so you only need to stand still and see His salvation, which He will accomplish for you (Exodus 14:13).

In teaching me what it means to have the Lord with you, God also showed me 2 Chronicles 20:17. It says, "You will not need to fight in this battle. Position yourselves, stand still and see the salvation of the Lord who is with you...Do not fear or be dismayed...for the Lord is with you." God told me, when the Lord is with you, you don't need to fight, the Lord will fight for you and you can hold your peace! Also, God promises, "No one will be able to stand against you all the days of your life. As I was with Moses, so I will be with you; I will never leave you nor forsake you" (Joshua 1:5). God is assuring us that He will personally fight for us and cause our enemies to fall because He is with us and He is for us (Romans 8). This is great news! I don't know about you, but I don't want to waste time fighting a defeated foe. My times are in the hands of God, and not to be used by a powerless devil via distractions. It is tempting to fight and defend ourselves, but because the Lord is with us, He fights for us, goes before us, and He is our defense (Deuteronomy 32:4, GNT). And we know that if God fights for us and defends us, we are defended and victorious!

God also showed me Psalm 91:15-16, which promises, "He shall call upon Me, and I will answer him, I will be with him in trouble; I will deliver him and honor him. With long life I will satisfy him and show him My salvation." Therefore, when God is with us, He is not with us to be a spectator, looking on our affliction. The Lord is with us to deliver us! Hallelujah! That would have been good enough for me, but God is so gracious to us and loves to give to us that He also promises He is with us to honor us, satisfy us with long life, and to show us His salvation (which is Yeshua, the name of Jesus, in Hebrew). God is very good to us!

Who knew that having the Lord with you could mean everything worth anything! Well, it did for Joseph, and if God made it so for Joseph, He will certainly do it for us! Again, God is not a respecter of persons, and indeed the Lord is with us. After all, God has promised: "I will never leave you nor forsake you" and all the promises of God in Christ are yes and in Him amen! (Deuteronomy 31:6).

What It Does Not Mean to Have the Lord with You

Sometimes understanding what something is not helps to truly know what it is. So let's look at what it does not mean to have the Lord with you. Having the Lord with you doesn't mean there will be an absence of trouble in your life. It doesn't mean that you will not be tested or tried. We see that truth also from the life of Joseph. He was betrayed by his own brothers, sold into slavery, falsely accused of a heinous crime he didn't commit, and thrown into prison because of it. Clearly, having the Lord with us doesn't mean afflictions won't come. In fact, the Bible says, "Many are the afflictions of the righteous but the Lord delivers him from them all" (Psalm 34:19). God wouldn't need to be our Deliverer unless there was something to deliver us from. But we see that through the life of Joseph that God did in fact deliver him from all of his troubles, and worked everything together for his good. In hindsight, looking at Joseph's life we can see the Lord was with him and for him, but this didn't stop the enemy from trying Joseph. It is important to note that the enemy didn't have something personally against Joseph, and his afflictions did not occur because of his own wrongdoing. It is vital that we know this because the devil seems to have mastered lying to people and telling them that the troubles in their life are their fault, or God's failure to help them, when the truth is that the devil is the one inflicting the pain. And Jesus has revealed in the scriptures the reason that the enemy persecutes us. Jesus explained it like this: "The sower sows the Word. And these are the ones by the wayside where the Word is sown. When they hear, Satan comes immediately and takes away the Word that was sown in their hearts. These likewise are the ones sown on stony ground who, when they hear the Word, immediately receive it with gladness; and they have no root in themselves, and so endure only for a time. Afterward, when **tribulation or persecution arises for the Word's sake**, immediately they stumble. Now these are the ones sown among thorns; they are ones who hear the Word, and the cares of the world, the deceitfulness of riches, and the desires for other things entering in choke the Word, and it becomes unfruitful. But these are ones sown on good ground, those who hear the Word, accept it, and bear fruit: some thirtyfold, some sixty, and some a hundred" (Mark 4:14-20). Therefore it is typical, as Jesus pointed out, that when God gives us a Word, Satan comes *immediately* to try to take that Word from us. This certainly happened to Joseph. God gave Joseph a dream...a destiny to fulfill, and hell was opposed to this dream coming to pass. Therefore it seemed like as soon as God gave the dreams the enemy went to work to try to stop it from coming to pass. We should know that the enemy is after the Word God gives, because when God gives a Word, God will certainly cause it to come to pass. When God gives a dream, He will certainly realize it! Even the devil knows this truth, which is why he works overtime to try to discourage the children of God, and weary them until the point that they give up and no longer believe God's Word of promise…or the dream He has placed in their hearts. When the enemy saw that the Lord was with Joseph, he tried all he could to stop Joseph from getting to his destiny, but we see that God in His infinite wisdom used every tactic of the devil to bring Joseph closer and closer to his dream until finally God caused Joseph to fulfill his entire destiny! God is doing the same thing today when the enemy comes against us; God is using every attack for our good, and for His glory, taking us into the fulfillment of every promise and our destiny! So although the Lord being with us doesn't mean we won't have trouble, it does mean God will deliver us from it, give us victory, and fulfill every promise He made us beyond what we asked or imagined!

Jesus Revealed

God has undoubtedly hidden Christ in the scriptures throughout the Old Testament. Jesus is revealed in the life of Joseph in ways that amaze me. It is important for us to take time and look at Jesus hidden in the life of Joseph, because God said that when we behold Jesus we are transformed into His very same image (2 Corinthians 3:18). We are not transformed by trying, but by beholding. Therefore, let us behold Jesus!

The Lord opened my eyes to see that Joseph is a type of Jesus Christ. Joseph was the beloved of his father, and Jesus is God's beloved in whom He is well pleased (Matthew 3:17). But like Jesus, Joseph was rejected and hated by his own brethren who betrayed Him, and in exchange for shekels of silver delivered Him up to the Gentiles (non-Jews). In Joseph's life, Joseph represents Jesus, and his brothers represent the Jewish nation that rejected Jesus when He came on the earth. Also, Joseph was falsely accused and sentenced for a crime he didn't commit. Likewise, our Lord was delivered up to the Chief Priest for a crime He didn't commit and sentenced according to injustice (Mark 15:10).

We also see Jesus hidden in the life of Joseph as it relates to the rejection of his own people but the acceptance of a gentile nation. Jesus came to the earth and was despised and rejected by his own people (Isaiah 53:3), but was accepted by the Gentiles who eventually became His bride (that's us, the church). Joseph, after being rejected and hated by his own, went to Egypt (representing a Gentile nation), where he was accepted and exalted by the Egyptians...and eventually married a Gentile bride (his Egyptian wife, a type of the church of Jesus Christ) (Romans 5:14).

We also see a futuristic parallel in the life of Joseph, which reveals Jesus' second coming. The Bible says that all of Israel will be saved (Romans 11:26). As demonstrated in the life of Joseph, we see that the second time Joseph's brethren came into Joseph's presence they recognized him and they bowed before him. And Joseph forgave them and saved them from perishing and lavished his love and provision on them. This is good news, because it reveals Jesus and His beautiful heart of love! When Jesus returns, the Jews will have their eyes opened and their blindness removed, and indeed all of Israel will be saved (Romans 11:26). They will acknowledge Jesus as the Messiah and they will experience God's grace as we Christians enjoy today! Indeed, God used Joseph to save both the Jews and the Gentiles, which is a clear picture of our Lord and Savior Jesus Christ, who is undoubtedly Savior of the world! God is so good and His heart is filled with love and tender mercies...and because we have just beheld Jesus, we have just been transformed into his very same image.

They Meant It for Evil; God Meant It for Good

I am convinced that the peace of God is not the absence of evil; it is resting at the table God prepared for us in the presence of our enemies (Psalm 23:5). The reason we can rest with enemies all around is because the Lord is with us…the Lord is for us…and even when someone means something for evil against us, God means it for your good! The Lord demonstrates His heart in this truth in Joseph's life as well. Without question, Joseph's brothers meant it for evil when they allowed their hate-filled hearts to decide to kill him, and only because of God's intervention did they settle for selling their own brother into slavery…and faking his death. But God meant all of it for good, and even used that level of darkness to save the life of many people, both Jews and Gentiles. God is the same yesterday, today, and forevermore. And that is why we can rest and trust God to take whatever was meant for evil and use it for our good!

Let Go and Let God!

God's nature and will for us is that we trust Him with our cares and concerns. Human nature seems to be to hold on for dear life to what we have…even problems. And when someone has suffered loss, the grip can get even tighter as they try to keep whatever is left because of the fear of losing more, or losing it all. But God's ways are better than our ways (Isaiah 55:8). God wants us to cast all of our cares on Jesus, because He cares for us, and it is His good pleasure and delight to bless us (1 Peter 5:7 & Psalm 35:27). There are great benefits and blessings for doing things God's way, which is why God has revealed and continues to reveal to us His ways. This is not for God's sake, it is for our own. The Bible says, that God's path drips with abundance (Psalm 65:11). God knows this truth, and that is why He tells us to follow Him in His ways…it leads to abundance as God has defined abundance! That has to be so much more than anything we can hope or ever imagine!

One of God's ways is that we let go and let God. In that way there is not only prosperity and abundance, but also rest for our souls (Psalm 65:11 & Matthew 11:29). This truth is demonstrated in many people's lives throughout the entire Bible, although we will only be looking a few of them here. Jacob's life clearly portrays this truth. As far as Jacob knew, had already lost Joseph, the son whom he dearly loved, and on top of that he had lost Rachel, Joseph's mom, who was the wife who Jacob loved most. Those are significant losses, so naturally when Jacob was told to let go of the other son he loved, Benjamin, who was also conceived by his favorite wife, his reaction was to refuse to let go and trust God. Namely, Jacob's older sons insisted that they take Benjamin down to Egypt with them in order to buy more grain from Joseph (who they didn't know was Joseph at the time), because Joseph instructed them to do so or they would be precluded from purchasing more grain. Jacob refused to let Benjamin go and risked everyone's life...including Benjamin's life. This leads me to the next point. Fear is absolutely blinding. Jacob was so fearful to let his son go and trust God because he didn't want his son to die, that he didn't realize he was guaranteeing his death by preventing him from getting more food in the famine! I can sympathize with Jacob, because I have had God tell me to let my children go and entrust them into His capable hands and care. It took years before I let go! Oh, but when I did, I knew freedom for real then. And whomever the Son of God sets free is free indeed (John 8:36). My children are in the Almighty hands of our loving Heavenly Father, and that is better than my hands any day. Well, finally, Jacob let go and let God, permitting them to take Benjamin to Egypt while saying, "If I am bereaved, I am bereaved" (Genesis 43:14). This leap of faith Jacob took led him to be reunited with his long-lost son,

Joseph, and it led him and his whole house to plenty of bread and a life of luxury during a famine! And by the way, Benjamin lived and was the most highly favored among all of Jacob's sons in Egypt! God is good, and He is worthy of our trust.

In the Bible, Queen Esther had to let go and let God also, when she faced almost certain death because she went to the king's chambers un-summoned by him, which carried a penalty of death unless the king pardoned her. Queen Esther risks her life by going before the king in order to plead for the life of her kinsmen, whose wrongful executions were imminently approaching. But Esther didn't let go immediately when God let her know He wanted her to go before the king. Her initial reaction was to seek to save her own life and pour out like water every excuse why she should not go. But eventually, and after being reminded of her God-given purpose, Queen Esther let go and let God saying, "If I perish, I perish" (Esther 4:16). The result of trusting God? Queen Esther lived, and she saved the life of her kinsman and saved the lives of an entire Jewish nation, while executing all of their enemies! Again, God is worthy of our trust.

Jesus is our greatest example of the power of letting go and letting God. The Bible says that Jesus loved not His life unto death (Philippians 2:8). He obeyed God even unto death. But remember, when Jesus came, He came in human flesh. Before Jesus was crucified, He prayed to God to pass that cup of suffering and sin He was about to drink for us. But He let go and let God, saying, "not My will but Your will be done" (Mark 13:42). And the result…just at the mention of His name every knee shall bow and every tongue shall confess that Jesus is Lord (Philippians 2:10). God is good and should be trusted!

Abraham was tested in like manner. God in demonstrating what He would do for us by delivering up Jesus for us, told Abraham to offer his only son as a sacrifice. Abraham had faith in God, figuring that even if God did allow him to kill his son, God could raise him from the dead. Abraham let go and let God. When he did this,

God called out to Abraham and told him not to slay his son. Thus, God spared Abraham's son from dying, even though God would not spare Himself this pain when He gave up His only begotten Son Jesus to die for us. Not only that, but God called Abraham to be the father of many nations, both Jews and Gentiles. God wasn't done. Abraham had been acknowledged by God Himself, as a man possessing faith and righteousness (Hebrews11:8 & Romans 4:16). God made sure He honored Abraham as a father, and that is the very area that Abraham surrendered to God. People of God, our Father changes not. What He did for them, He will do for us. When we let go and let God, we are trusting God and when we trust God, we will never by any means be put to shame, but we will be exalted by the hand of Almighty God! Therefore, whatever the issue you are facing, let go and let God and like the children of God who came before you; you will not regret it but will be greatly blessed!

In Closing

We have been blessed to see what it means to have the Lord with us, and God, who cannot lie, has reassured us that He is with us and will never leave us. Jesus promised, "I am with you always, even to the end of the age" (Matthew 28:20). Therefore, all the favor, promises, provision, divine protection, success, and all the blessings that come when the Lord is with you, are our portion both now and forevermore. God put the life of Joseph in the Bible for us to not only know this truth, but to believe it, declare it, and watch it manifest in every area of our lives!

Fear not, for I am with you; be not dismayed, for I am your God. (Isaiah 41:10)

CHAPTER 2:

GOD IS FIGHTING FOR YOU!

You will not need to fight in this battle. Position yourselves, stand still and see the salvation of the
Lord, who is with you. (2 Chronicles 20:17)

To say that Moses' life got off to a rocky start is an understatement! From the time he was in his mother's womb, the devil himself put a hit out on him via an evil king, Pharaoh. At that time Pharaoh ruled over all of Egypt where Moses' Israelite kinsmen lived as slaves (Exodus 1). During this same time, Moses parents conceived him and the enemy used this unjust king to issue a decree that ordered every newborn male child to be cast into a river to die (Exodus 1:22). Notably, Pharaoh did this because he feared that someday these Israelites would become so great in number they would join forces with his enemies, overthrow him, and leave out of Egypt (Exodus1:9). You see, you have no business being afraid of the enemy; he is afraid of you. More accurately, he is afraid of the One, Jesus Christ, who lives on the inside of you, and is for you. This is almost always a cause as to why the enemy attacks you: He has discovered that as vicious as his assaults have been against you, you are still standing, and God is still multiplying you, the same way he caused Moses and his people to stand and continue multiplying!

God Knows How to Hide You

Although this decree had been issued, the Bible says Moses' mother, after giving birth to him, "when she saw that he was a beautiful child, she hid him for three months." Afterwards, she could no longer hide him, however. Moses' mom then did what we all should do, she let go and entrusted the life of her beautiful baby boy to God, knowing that what she could not do, God would. She trusted God with the life of her son, and God indeed proved Himself loving, powerful, and faithful to protect the child and even restore him to his mother. (Parents, God is speaking to us right now).

After she let Moses go in her heart, the Lord led her to make an ark for him and daub it with both asphalt and pitch (Exodus 2:3). Now, God showed me this ark, and the ark God built through Noah are both pictures of Jesus Christ for the Christian today. Today, the Christian is in Christ...the Ark. The Bible says, "And God raised us up with Christ and seated us with Him in the heavenly realms **in Christ Jesus** (Ephesians 2:26), and when God seated Jesus, together with us in Him, God "seated Him at His right hand...far above all principality and power and might and dominion, and every name that is named, not only in this age but also in that which is to come" (Ephesians 1:21). This is where we, the children of God, are today; we are seated in Jesus Christ, our Ark, in heavenly places far above all evil! And we can see what divine protection God provides us by placing us in Christ, our Ark, by looking into Moses' life. After Moses' mom put him in the ark, she placed him into the very same river the enemy ordered all the male babies be thrown into so that they would surely die. This right here tells us that even if we are in what seems to be enemy territory; God will protect us and work everything together for our good. God is not always a God of prevention, but He is always a God of divine protection. Moses was in a river not knowing how to swim to avoid drowning, or how to preclude any of the crocodiles in that river from eating him, but God protected him and he was totally safe inside the ark. Likewise—but even more so today—God has placed the believer in Jesus Christ, and therefore even if death is surrounding us and we don't know how to protect ourselves, we are completely safe in Christ Jesus.

Notably, the Lord not only protected Moses but also directed his path, causing that river to turn Moses in the direction God ordained for him to go in (Exodus 2). Sometimes we may not realize it, but God is ordering our steps (Proverbs 16:9). The Bible then says that Moses' sister stood afar off to see what would happen to the boy (Exodus 2). What she saw next I believe changed her life forever. God caused the river to turn its course, pushing Moses along the riverbank right into the backyard, so to speak, of the evil king's palace and into the arms of his daughter. The Bible says, clearly this woman knew that the baby was a Hebrew (the race of children to be killed pursuant to the king's decree), but instead of having him killed, "she had compassion on him," had Moses drawn out of the deadly water, took him in as her own son, and placed him right underneath the same roof as the evil king who wanted to execute him! Children of God, this is apparent: God is in control!

God then caused this evil king to take care of Moses, and provide the choicest food, clothing, shelter, and education to him (the very one he desired to kill). Don't worry if people have purposed in their hearts to destroy you. God won't allow them to take you down, but He may make them take you out…to lunch that is! God has a sense of humor I'm telling you! And indeed, God knows how to hide us from the enemy, even if it's right under his nose. I suppose Moses' parents may have felt some level of fear knowing their Israelite infant boy was in the house of a serial killer of Jewish baby boys. But like them, we too, can rest in and fully trust the wisdom of our God. God knew that the enemy would not even think to look for a Hebrew slave in his Egyptian palace, so that is where He hid Moses for His divine purpose and His people whom He loved. I marvel at the infinite wisdom and unfailing love of our Lord Jesus Christ!

From the Desert to Destiny

One day, after Moses had become an adult, he observed the wicked and evil ways the Egyptians of that time treated his Hebrew people, and understandably he despised it. Moses, however, hated it so much that after witnessing the beating of one of his people, he became enraged and killed the Egyptian who had beaten his brethren (Exodus 2:11). The indignation that Moses must have felt about the treacherous way his people were being treated was without question a righteous indignation. The problem was not Moses' anger, but that he had not allowed God to fight for him and his loved ones, and instead sought to avenge his brethren himself. As a result, Moses found himself in serious trouble, fleeing Egypt for his life as a wanted fugitive for murder. There is a valuable lesson here for all of us, because we have all likely been faced with serious forms of injustice that produce a holy and just indignation. However, if this indignation is not comingled with the fact that "the battle is the Lord's" (2 Chronicles 20:15) and God will fight for us and defend us things can go from really bad too much worse. I learned this in my own life. It's simply better to allow God to fight for you, because when God vindicates, nobody can bring any charge against Him; and if they tried, it would be futile! If we, however, try to vindicate ourselves we could very well end up in a world of trouble like Moses did.

Moses, I believe at that time, lacked a revelation of who God was in His life, and in the lives of His people, and because of that lack of knowledge, that God fights for His own, Moses found Himself a fleeing felon in the desert. Now, some might call this situation Moses got himself into rock bottom, because in Egypt he likely ate the choicest cuisine, wore the finest of clothes, and obtained the highest of educations, but here he ended up in the desert. But God! God used what looked like rock bottom—the desert where nothing really grows, and it's dry, empty and lonely —as a launching pad for Moses to begin fulfilling his destiny. Someone reading this may be in what seems like a desert right now. God wants you to know that there is hope for you, even if you did something to cause or contribute to the desert-like circumstance. The Lord doesn't want you to despair, because God changes not, and as He was with Moses, as we will soon see, so is He with you and me (Hebrews 13:8). God is not a respecter of persons. What the Lord did for Moses, He will do for us. Always remember that God is faithful both in the waters (like when Moses was completely innocent, and did nothing to avail himself of the situation he was in), and God is faithful in the desert, the driest of places (like when Moses' own decision caused him to be in the predicament he was in).

So whether you've behaved like an angel, or an assailant, God is faithful and will never by any means leave or forsake you. The Bible makes this truth very plain. God is faithful even if we are unfaithful (2 Timothy 2:13). And God promises, "I will be with him in trouble; I will deliver him and honor him" (Psalm 91:15). God showed me a truth in this verse one day while spending time with Him that has deeply blessed me; He is with us in trouble, and never said His presence or promise to help us depends on who caused the trouble we got into. I was liberated when God showed me this truth! We can truly rest knowing that even when we make mistakes, the same loving God who was with Moses in the waters, and in the desert, is with us too, wherever we go and no matter what we've done (Joshua 1:9).

Not only is God with us, but God is for us, to make sure He accomplishes the plan He has for us, and to make sure that nothing, and nobody, thwarts His plan...including ourselves (Romans 8:31-32 & Job 42:2). Indeed, the Lord was for Moses, too. It was in the desert that God met with Moses face to face, so to speak, and revealed Himself to Moses personally. This dry place is where Moses was privileged to get to know God for Himself. It was in a desert place that I was blessed to get to know God for myself too. My life changed drastically, and all for the better, right in the middle of that desert. Notably, the desert is also where God revealed to Moses the purpose for which He created him, and delivered him from fear in order to fulfill his God-given destiny. This too, is what happened to me. In the desert place, God began to unveil to me my destiny. Also like Moses, I had to first be delivered from fear in order to embrace my destiny...and it was in the desert that the deliverance took place (Exodus 3). This is why as children of God, even if in the desert place, we need not fear or despair; God is for us and not even the driest and most lifeless thing can be against us! Jesus, too, was driven into the wilderness (Mark 1:12). But because of God's unfailing love for Him, Jesus went from the wilderness to walking on water as if it were solid ground! (Matthew14:22-33). This same Abba Father of Jesus' is your Abba Father, too! Now, it's worth noting that Moses' mistake led him into the wilderness, and Jesus, who is without sin, was driven by the Spirit of God into the wilderness, but God was with and for them both, and this same loving God is with and for us, whether the Spirit led us there or we led ourselves.

In the desert, God showed Moses how He called him to be an instrument in God's own hand to deliver God's children from their oppressors. I love how God works all things together for our good! God is so rich in mercy. He was turning Moses' mistake into one miracle after another. By the way, in case someone is wondering did God do anything that blessed Moses practically (his natural needs or desires) while in the desert, the answer is that indeed He did. God is

Spirit, but He understands we have both spiritual and natural needs and desires; and the Lord loves to satisfy them both! While in the desert, God gave Moses shelter, a wife, children, and a new family who loved him! I'm so encouraged right now, and I know you are too! Our God is a mighty river in the desert (Isaiah 43:19).

Now, God in revealing who He was to Moses, and the plan He had for his life, has also revealed His heart for us, His children. The Bible says that God "heard [His children's] groaning" and "remembered His covenant" (Exodus 2:24). God always keeps, and remembers His covenant. And God remembers His covenant with Jesus, made on our behalf, and for our benefit (Hebrews 8:6-13). Jesus is seated at God's right hand in Heaven reminding God by His very risen presence of what God promised to do for us, after Christ was beaten, bled, and then died for us on the cross in our place, and afterwards was raised from the dead for our justification (Romans 4:25). And in this new covenant God promises for the ones who believe on Christ, He has forgiven all your sins, justified you (made you righteous in His sight), and given you an inheritance to share with Jesus Christ Himself, that is filled with endless blessings and benefits, including health, wealth, and peace! So if for any reason you don't feel worthy of God or His blessings, you must know that Jesus is worthy and deserving, and you and Christ are one (Galatians 2:20). Beloved, as Jesus is, so are you in this world (1 John 4:17). Christ is worthy, blameless, powerful, seated far above principalities and darkness, rich beyond measure, whole, complete, blessed, and so much more, and therefore, so are you in this world. God remembers His new covenant with Christ for our sakes, hears our cry and will fulfill every promise He made us pursuant to it.

Then God, further revealing His heart for His children, said to Moses, what He is saying to some of us today, "I have surely *seen* the oppression of My people…and have *heard* their cry…for I *know* their sorrows. So *I have come* down *to deliver them*" (Exodus 3:7-8). Notice how God *sees* what His people are going through, *hears* our cry, *knows* any sorrow we have, and *comes to deliver us!* You can rest knowing without any doubt that God has heard your cry, seen the oppression against you, knows the sorrows you have felt, and has come to deliver you. Your deliverance is certain and has been promised by God Himself. The Lord also showed me this truth when looking at this same passage of scripture: He has already come to deliver us! This means, the Lord has already come into the situation that opposes you, to deliver you. This is good news!

Another thing the Lord blessed me to see was that God promised He had come Himself to deliver His children. The Lord then began to show me how some of His people have become discouraged because their own efforts to try to deliver themselves, or their loved ones, have proved futile, causing them frustration. The Lord doesn't want His people frustrated; He wants us in His peace knowing that He is the Deliverer, and that He will deliver His people. You will soon see that the children of Israel were not responsible for their deliverance. God made the promise to deliver them, and God kept the promise by coming Himself to deliver. The same is true for us today. God is our Deliverer, and He has come Himself to deliver us, we just gotta let Him finish.

Now, before we move on to look at the next phase of Moses' life in order to learn more about the Lord and His love for us, I want to share with you something else Jesus taught me about His ways while studying Moses' life. The Lord revealed to me that He will sometimes take His chosen children out of a place, and even away from family for a time, in order to deliver them from whatever is hindering them, in order to reveal Himself to them, and show them their destiny. Afterwards He sends them back into that same place they came out of in order to fulfill it. Yes, the Lord will take you out, in order to take things out of you, fill you up with what you need to fulfill your destiny, and bring you back in for His purpose. God did it with Moses. The Lord revealed Himself to Moses, and His plan for Moses' life after he was out of Egypt and away from his people. God spoke to

Moses and told him what His plan for his life was to send Moses back into Egypt, because God had come to deliver His people there, and He was going to use Moses in this process. Now, the Lord does not send us back into a place to conform to that environment, or indulge in the evil lusts therein, but He does send us to co-labor with Christ in order to deliver the rest of His children.

It happened to me in my own life. I was completely and suddenly uprooted from the arena I had become accustomed to (a life filled with what the world calls "the rich and famous"). Suddenly I found myself alone with God, away from family, and void of any friends, and there were days where I didn't even go outside. I was not depressed, I was in a desert place, and surely that was where God revealed Himself to me and His plan for my life, as well as delivered me in order to fulfill my destiny...which involved going back into that same arena to co-labor with Christ in order to deliver His people. But notably, when God began to tell me it was time to leave the desert, I was so accustomed to it that I didn't want to leave. I made all kind of excuses to God why I should just stay put where I was in the desert. Moses had this same hesitation. He told God all the reasons he could come up with, why he should not leave the desert and go back to Egypt...including the fact that he stuttered (Exodus 4:10). God had to show Moses what He had to reveal to me about fulfilling our God-given destinies: The very power of God will rest upon you, and it won't be you accomplishing this, but it will be Me (Exodus 4:3). And God had to do this because I was like Moses; I was comfortable in complacency. But God encouraged me, like He did Moses, and drew me out of the desert into fulfilling my destiny for His glory, and the good of a multitude of His people. So beloved, if you are in a desert place, don't get comfortable there, because God is surely taking you from the desert to your destiny!

God's Word is More Than Enough!

Once God convinced Moses to trust Him and head back to Egypt with Him, the Lord explained to Moses that this wicked king wasn't going to let God's children go out of Egypt initially, but that God Himself would have to come and strike this enemy in order for him to let God's children go (Exodus 3). At this point Moses had what a lot of believers have from their Heavenly Father: A Word (a promise) from God. A Word from God may not seem like much, but it is more than enough. This, my friends, is where the battle really begins; what God calls the good fight of faith (1 Timothy 6:12). Jesus showed me clearly that this battle arises for the Word's sake (Mark 4:17). As evidenced in the life of Moses, soon after he received that Word from God, that God promised to set the Israelites free from bondage and bring them into a blessed land of their own that flows with milk and honey, the persecution against them increased like never before. By then Moses, along with his brother Aaron, had also gone before the Pharaoh and told him what God said: "Let My people go" (Exodus 5:1). At this point, the promise of God had been made known to the children of God, and they believed it, but it had also been made known to the enemy. Therein lies the reason for the raging storm that arose. The enemy seemed to become increasingly evil, and began to persecute these people in ways they had never suffered before. The Pharaoh increased their laborious toil, but decreased the materials they needed to complete the work, commanding that they still meet the same deadline for making his bricks, or suffer his physical violence against them and their loved ones (Exodus 5:7). Of course, this was "mission impossible," and therefore they were not able to do this, and they were beaten (Exodus 5:13-14).

The enemy wasn't angry with them, but had a problem with what God said. The same is true today, and Jesus explains why the enemy brings these storms or persecutions in the book of Mark (4:14-20). Like previously stated, the enemy wants to steal the Word

God gave you. Jesus even tells us what the enemy uses to steal the Word from people: for some he uses the cares (worries) of this world; for others, he uses the lust of riches; and for some, he uses persecution to try to get them to doubt God and give up their promise from the Lord (Mark 4:14-20). Jesus then showed me that the enemies' tactics actually bears witness that God will do everything He promised you. The Lord went on and explained to me that, "the enemy wouldn't bother My people after they get a promise from Me unless he knew that I will surely keep My promises" (Deuteronomy 7:9). Jesus showed me that the devil actually believes God will do what He promises, and that is why when God promised in the Garden of Eden that the seed of the woman (Eve) would crush the head of the serpent, the devil went on a desperate rampage trying to stop God, beginning with influencing Cain to kill Abel, all the way to ordering all male infants to be killed during the time Jesus was born, who indeed crushed his head (John 19:2). You see, the devil isn't after us, he is after the Word. The enemy doesn't want us to believe God, even though he does, and he wants us to doubt God, even though he doesn't! You and I have to know that no matter what persecution or temptation the enemy sends against us, God is faithful and will absolutely do everything He promised well above anything we could ever pray for, hope, or imagine (Ephesians 3:20). We must not lose hope in Jesus, but even if we have, it is still not too late for God to do all He promised us.

Jesus revealed to me His unfailing faithfulness by looking at a prominent event that took place in the life of His disciples who walked with Him. One day Jesus spoke to His disciples and gave them a Word, telling them they were going to the other side of the lake (Mark 4:35). After Jesus gave them that Word, He got in the boat with His disciples and a great storm rose up against them...and it did for the Word's sake. The disciples' reaction to the storm, despite the Word they were just given from Jesus, was that they became exceedingly fearful and questioned the Lord's love and care for them.

"Teacher, do You not care that we are perishing?" they asked Jesus. Now, Jesus had just told them they were going to cross over, but when that storm, the persecution, arose for the Word's sake, the disciples forgot what Jesus promised, became fearful and falsely accused Jesus of not caring for them. Jesus, unmoved by the waves, water, or wind, lay sound asleep on that boat, but even at the accusatory cry of His children the Lord arose and rebuked the entire storm...and with a Word! Yes, again Jesus gave His Word! And His Word was more than enough! Jesus was never asleep because He didn't care what happened to them, because Jesus loved them like He loves us... and so much so that He laid down His life for us. Jesus was asleep because He knew the sovereign Word He spoke was going to accomplish what He sent it to do...take them to the other side! Jesus knew then what He is teaching us today: The Word from God will get you what you need and where you need to be! It was never the responsibility of the disciples to get them to the other side, nor did Jesus rely on the absence of opposition to get them to the other side; His faith was in His sovereign Word! Neither the presence nor absence of the storm could stop the Word from coming to pass because the Word came from God Himself! Jesus didn't rebuke that storm either because it had any power to stop His Word; He rebuked it for His children's sake, because He knew they were filled with fear. Jesus knew all along that the Word alone would sustain them! That is why Jesus spoke the Word before they even embarked on the boat. The Lord knows all things, and knows what storm or persecutions the enemy will cause to arise, and that is why God sends the Word ahead of the storm. The Lord knew for them, what He knows for us today: The Word will take us safely to the other side! This is why Jesus could sleep sound and unafraid while hell gave its best shot! I pray we have this revelation of the power of a Word from God.

Now, Jesus not only spoke to this storm causing it to cease, but He spoke to His children too, like He is speaking to some of us: "Why are you so fearful? How is it that you have no faith?" Jesus asked this because He had given His Word and was with them in that boat. How were they going to perish when resurrection life itself was with them! Also, why were they fearful, when the Lord Himself spoke to them and made them a promise? Surely no storm or persecution gives reason to be afraid, because there is no storm or persecution that could ever stop the Word of God! God speaks and it is so! Thankfully, regardless of their lack of faith in what Jesus said, Jesus remained faithful, and He got them to the other side just like He promised. Jesus is good! The Lord is indeed faithful, even if we are faithless. And the love and faithfulness He showed His disciples then, is the same love and faithfulness He shows us today... even if we lose faith in Him, because Jesus is the same yesterday, today, and forever.

Someone reading this may only have a Word from God, and everything else can seem like winds and tempest against them, but Jesus Himself assures you today: If a Word from God is all you have, a Word from God is all you need, no matter whatever, or whomever, tries to come against you! Beloved, don't be fearful of a foe that is already defeated, and don't doubt Jesus' love for you or His absolute faithfulness! Remember, even if you are faithless, the Lord remains faithful. God cannot deny Himself, and He is His Word, and He promised when His Word goes out of His mouth, it will never return back void or empty, but it shall accomplish what He pleases and it shall prosper in the thing for which He sent it (Isaiah 55:11). People, our God reigns, and He alone is sovereign! The Lord alone is God, and besides Him there is no other God! There is not a created thing that can stop the Word of God...because again...God is His Word, and nothing and nobody can stop God! When God gets ready to move, He moves! God is moving right now on your behalf, because this unstoppable God is your Father and He loves you! This same Jesus who was calm in that storm with the disciples is calm when a storm arises against us, because Jesus walks by faith and not by reasoning. The disciples reasoned...the boat's rocking, the wind's blowing and the heavy rain is falling…there is but one conclusion… we're going down! What they thought and said was reasonable, but it was void of faith. Jesus, refusing to reason, instead walked by faith and was thus able to rebuke the winds, the rain, the waves, and shut the whole storm down with **one** Word; Shalom! (Mark 4:39).

They had reasoning and it filled them with fear and stripped them of any power to do anything about the storm they were in. Reasoning always precedes and produces doubt and fear…and fear can be literally paralyzing. And while reasoning may make sense to the human mind, reasoning doesn't make miracles, which is what a lot of us are praying for. I don't know about you, but I don't need intellect; I need intervention…divine intervention from God Himself! Let us follow after Jesus and renounce to reasoning in the things of God once and for all…and watch doubt utterly fall! Let us imitate Jesus and walk by faith instead of sight. We cannot do both. Faith and reasoning are antagonistic of one another. Reasoning says, if it doesn't make sense, it will never be made. Faith says, if it doesn't make sense, it makes miracles! Reasoning says why it can never happen. Faith says it is already finished! Reasoning is rooted in pride, believing what it thinks to be true, while counting the promise of God as foolishness. Faith is the greatest manifestation of humility, forsaking all human intellect and relying only on what our sovereign God says! Reasoning says, if I cannot figure it out, it isn't possible. Faith says, surely with God all things are possible, and God doesn't need my understanding to be a condition precedent to His promise being fulfilled in my life! Reasoning lives in the realm of the senses, where whatever can be seen, heard, or felt is true. Faith lives in the heavenly realm, knowing that whatever God said is true! Faith triumphs over reasoning every time. God said it is foolishness to those who are perishing, but it is **the power of God** for those who believe! (1 Corinthians 1:18). God always puts to shame and resists reasoning (human wisdom and logic) because it's rooted in pride (1 Corinthians 1:19). The Lord, however, supplies grace to the humble and honors those who believe in Him (1 Peter 5:5). Remember, the Word of God says, "few of you were wise in the world's eyes or powerful or wealthy when God called you. Instead, God chose things the world considers foolish in order to shame those who think they are wise. And he chose things that are powerless to shame those who are powerful. God chose things despised by the world; things counted as nothing at all, and used them to bring to nothing what the world considers important. As a result, no one can ever boast in the presence of God" (1 Corinthians 1:26-29). These are the ways of our wise God!

Moses believed God, and the Word of God says, "Moses was **very humble,** more than all men who were on the face of the earth (Numbers 12:3). The Lord spoke to Moses and promised Him things that were clearly impossible for any human to accomplish, but Moses still believed God...and was declared, not just humble, but "very humble" Now, this doesn't mean Moses was perfect in his faith in God. Only Jesus alone can claim honestly to have perfect faith in God. Moses struggled with faith, and doubted God when persecution arose for the Word's sake just like Jesus' disciples did that night in the boat, and like I have so many times I don't have a count, and like many of you may have, too. But thanks be to God who remains faithful, even if we are faithless! The Lord certainly remained faithful to Moses and the children of Israel even after doubting His promise. After the enemy increased their burdens and began to violently abuse them, Moses went to the Lord and cried "Lord, why have You brought trouble on this people? For since I came to Pharaoh to speak in Your name, [speak the Word God spoke to him,] he has done evil to this people; neither have You delivered Your people at all" (Exodus 5:22-23, Emphasis Mine).

Notice how Moses believed that the Lord had brought the trouble on the people. God had not beaten them, it was God who promised to deliver them from that evil bondage; but Moses, like the disciples and me as well, blamed God when hell seemed to break loose in his life. The Lord's response to Moses is what it is to us today. The Lord, very lovingly and patiently, reassured Moses that He will surely deliver on His promise to bring His children out of bondage and into the promised land He swore to give to their father Abraham (Exodus 6). God spoke His promise to them again for their sake. When God spoke the first time, His Word was powerful enough to deliver His people and bring them into the promised land, but God is merciful and so He will confirm to us as many times as are needed so that we are encouraged on our way to our specific "promised land"—so to speak—that He promises us today. You may have wondered why God confirms His Word to you more than once. It is to help you fight the good fight of faith, because that is your only fight beloved. Moses and the children of Israel were never called by God to fight against the enemy, for it was God who would fight for them, but they did have to fight the good fight of faith…and as we believers all have to do the same. In other words, we have to let God finish. Now, it wasn't long after this that God's Word began to manifest in their lives in a very tangible way! Faith in God will not be disappointed; and the Word of God will never fail. God's Word is always more than enough!

God Is Vindicating You

After the Lord reassured Moses and His people that God will surely bring them out of bondage, interestingly He told him that He would harden Pharaoh's heart and that Pharaoh would not heed the directive from God to let His people go (Exodus 7). The Lord in His infinite wisdom knew that Pharaoh was someone who would never stop trying to bind and afflict these people in all his pride and arrogance, and therefore God would have to lay His hand on him and all of Egypt and execute great judgments against this adversary. The pride that Pharaoh was so engrossed in that he refused to listen to God Himself became very apparent after God began to send one plague after another against this wicked king who still continued to hold His children captive and abuse them.

The Lord set out to perform His first miraculous sign in the form of a plague through Moses. First, the Lord touched their water source, turning it from water to blood. Now, don't fear, sons and daughters of God, because Jesus has died for all your sins and took all your punishment and judgment upon Himself at the cross, thus turning our water into wine...not blood! (John 2:1-11). Now, all of Egypt was without any water, but this prideful Pharaoh was just destined to fall, so indeed he continued in refusing to do what God said (Exodus 7). Therefore, God sent Moses again and warned Pharaoh that if he didn't let God's people go, He was going to smite all the territory of Egypt with frogs. Needless to say, he didn't listen and as a result, frogs were everywhere, even on the people of Egypt. Bothered by this, Pharaoh asked Moses to pray to the Lord so that the frogs would go away, and then he would let God's people go. This too, my friends, is pure pride! I don't know what made this man believe that God really needed his permission to set His own people free! But pride will do that; it will cause someone to abandon all wisdom. The earth is the Lord's and the fullness therein (Psalm 24:1). But evidently Pharaoh didn't understand that. Everything was created by God and for His glory, and when God gets ready to take something back that belongs to Him, no one and nothing can stop Him. This foolish Pharaoh was just a man, whose breath is in his nostrils, but clearly he thought he was god. It was God who created Pharaoh, not the other way around. It was God who raised Pharaoh up and allowed him to become the king, so that the power of God may be made known throughout all the earth (Romans 9:17). And it would be God to take this false god down! The same is true for any false gods that have risen against you in your life; God will surely make them all utterly fall! God is sovereign, and He is God all by Himself, and besides Him there is no other (Isaiah 45:5). We have to remember this truth people of God, when the enemy comes against us. The enemy, and mankind acting as his agent, are merely the creation of an all-powerful Creator who is on your side. Sons and daughters of God, you are loved and you are protected, and surely the Lord fights for you!

Despite this truth, Pharaoh was destined for doom and therefore, after the Lord removed the frogs, Pharaoh still refused to let God's children go. Well, the Lord doesn't get tired or weary, so He sent yet another plague against this wicked man and all his people (Exodus 8:16). This time, lice. At this point Pharaoh acknowledged that this was "the finger of God," but his heart was plagued with hardness and pride, and he refused to let God's people go (Exodus 8:18-19).

And again, God sent Moses to announce to the hard-hearted ruler that another plague was headed his way. This time, God sent thick swarms of flies on His enemies and their land, corrupting the entire land, but the Lord "set apart" the land where His children lived, making a difference between Pharaoh's people and God's people. The enemies' response to the judgment of God then, was the same as it is today; he lied and he tried…lied to God's children and tried God as if He wasn't God all by Himself. Indeed, Pharaoh told Moses that if he would pray to God to take the flies away, he would let God's people go BUT they couldn't go far; they would have to stay in the land and worship God. This, my friends, is a picture of perfect pride! Pharaoh really believed that he could give God a counter-offer, and initiate negotiations with God about His own children being free! Beloved, perhaps the enemy has come against you with this negotiation tactic, purporting to have any negotiating power, and offered you some illusive freedom, but not the total freedom that Jesus promised you. Let's look at our God's response, because as it was then, so it is today in our lives, when the enemy engages in his desperate attempts to modify what God said. The Lord sent another plague against His enemy! This time it was **very severe** pestilence sent on all of Pharaoh's livestock (Exodus 9:3). That is still the Lord's response to whatever has tried to keep you, and your loved ones, captive...offering to loosen up your chains, but not release you as God has commanded. And that's because what the enemy offers is the equivalent to giving a prisoner a larger jail cell; the prisoner is still a bound, and the extra square footage is only intended to pacify the prisoner so they continue to live under this mirage of freedom. The enemy wants us to think, "Prison isn't so bad!" Lies! Prison is terrible. That is why when someone commits even the most heinous of crimes, like rape and murder, out of all the places judges can put them, and out of all the punishment that can be executed against them, the judge orders that sentence be that they are put in prison...a form of bondage. Bondage is bad. This is why Jesus came to set the captives free (Luke 4:18). So whether the enemy has tried to put you into a prison of guilt, condemnation, addiction, depression, poverty, or any other form of bondage, the Lord is present to set the captives free and Jesus isn't making deals with the devil! Either the enemy lets you go, or he loses his life...and you still go free! Jesus is serious about His bride, and we are the bride of Christ. Now, this plague the Lord sent against their livestock was serious back then, because livestock was a crucial means of obtaining wealth during those times, and represented wealth itself in many respects. So today, this would be the equivalent to God striking your enemies' finances and drying them up. But again, like God showed us, Pharaoh was destined for disaster, and therefore, he refused to heed God's Word and let His children go.

Thus, the Lord sent boils on all the Egyptians, and the magicians Pharaoh had used to help him do evil, and they couldn't even stand before Moses because of the severity of the boils on them (Exodus 9:11). And then the Lord sent "very heavy hail to rain down, such as has not been in Egypt since its founding" (Exodus 9:23). This

was an unprecedented judgment God released against those hold-
ing His children captive. This caused Pharaoh to call for Moses and
exclaim, "I have sinned *this time*. The Lord is righteous, and my people and I are wicked" (Exodus 9:27). Wow! Pride and foolishness
go hand and hand. This evil ruler said he had sinned *this time*! So
executing the innocent infant boys and beating nearly to death God's
children wasn't sin to him. But denying God *this time*…he counted
as a sin. Let us all just acknowledge and accept right now that there
are some people who the Lord Himself knows are filled with pride,
hardened in their hearts, refusing to allow God to save them and
therefore utter destruction is their destiny. The Lord knew this about
Pharaoh from the beginning, which is why He told Moses, "I am
sure that the king of Egypt will not let you go, no, not even by a
mighty hand. So I will stretch out My hand and strike Egypt with all
My wonders which I will do in its midst" (Exodus 3:19). Moses was
surely given understanding of this truth from God; God knows from
the beginning what everyone's end will be. So when Pharaoh asked
Moses to pray for him that the Lord would remove the plague, and
lied, saying he would let the people of God go, Moses responded,
"But as for you and your servants, I know that you will not yet fear
the Lord God." Moses knew for sure that Pharaoh would deny God,
but He also knew for sure God would deliver His people. And as an
added bonus, on the way to receiving their miracle from God, He
was vindicating them concerning their enemies. Now, albeit this was
true, in order to be free they had to let God finish!

Afterwards, the Lord sent locusts upon Pharaoh and his people. The plague was so severe that it covered the face of the earth, so
that no one was able to see (Exodus 10:15). This time the Egyptians
got wise and they went to Pharaoh to tell him that he needed to let
God's children go because Egypt was destroyed, but pride doesn't
take heed to wisdom, and surely if Pharaoh wouldn't heed the Lord's
voice, he wasn't going to follow the directions of any man. So this
time, Pharaoh lied, saying he would let God's children go, in this

manner: "The Lord had better be with you when I let you and your little ones go! Beware, for evil is ahead of you" (Exodus 10:10). The enemy is doing this same thing today, too: When negotiating fails, he uses fear…because fear is also a form of bondage. Notice how the means used to release fear was in the form of a threat. God told me one day, "Fearful people use threats." By then, Pharaoh was afraid, and tried to mask that fear with idle threats. The enemy likely has come against you with that same tactic—empty threats, hoping that you will fear him, so that his fear of you will be alleviated. But whether you fear him or not, what he fears will never cease, because it isn't coming from you; this vindication is coming from God and God always finishes what He begins! (Isaiah 66:9).

So if the devil is threating you, a lot of times through people— like he operated through Pharaoh—it is a manifestation of his fear of you! More accurately, he is terrified of the One who lives on the inside of you, Jesus Christ! God has done to your enemies what He did to Moses and the children of Israel's enemies; He has made you a god to them! And this is why they are afraid of you and threaten you hoping to bind you with fear…they think that the plagues sent against them are from you. But sons and daughters of God, we know the truth; those plagues are from the Lord. So whether you are bound or free, shaking in your boots or confident in Christ, the Lord won't stop those plagues until you are free as He promised! The enemy to this day still fails to realize that it is God sending the plagues; and the Lord is doing the fighting because it is Him who promised you the freedom.

Now, it is important to note that the children of God who were held captive as slaves were not there to see the plagues that the Lord sent against their enemies, but nevertheless God was vindicating them, and likewise God is vindicating, us too, even if you don't see the Lord plaguing the one who has come against you. It is equally important to understand that God is fighting for us, and He has a perfect plan to deliver us out of bondage, and bring us into the promised land of abundance, and this is true even if what God is doing doesn't seem to be changing the enemy. The Lord sent one plague after another against Pharaoh, and he remained hard in his heart, unwilling to change, and neither did he let God's people go. The Lord showed me that some of His children have wanted to give up because they think that in order to be free their captor—this enemy who has held them hostage—has to change, or be in agreement with what God promised. This simply isn't true. God will do what He promised you even if those who have come against you never change! And God certainly doesn't need them to agree with Him. God told me plainly one day, I don't need the one coming against you to agree with Me in order for Me to do what I promised you. Absolutely liberating! That's what I have to say about this truth that God revealed that day! This is because I used to believe that those that came against me had to change their ways or repent in order for me to be free from their persecution or bondage, or receive what God promised me. It was despairing because no matter what plague of judgment the Lord sent, their hearts remained hard. The Lord has blessed me to understand that some of His enemies will never truly repent, or change their ways…they are, like Pharaoh, destined for destruction. So know children of God that whether the enemy who has come against you goes down after one plague, or ten plagues, God will do all He promised you and the Lord is vindicating you!

The Difference Between Israel and Egypt

During the time when the Lord was releasing His judgment in Egypt, He strategically placed Moses and all His people in Goshen and protected them and their possessions from the judgment that He released. This is relevant for us today, and its very good news! Goshen is a type of Jesus Christ. Today, as Christians, Jesus is our Goshen, and in Him we are safe, even from the judgment of God.

This isn't because we haven't done any wrong; it is because Jesus took upon Himself all of our sins at the cross where the judgment of God was released against Him in our stead. And in turn, Jesus gave us His place—a place of His righteousness—so that all the blessings of God would come upon us (2 Corinthians 5:21). This display of perfect obedience at the cross that Jesus did for our sake, dying in our place, fulfilling all the righteous requirement of God's law for us (Romans 8:4), and giving us His righteousness, has made us "heirs of God, and joint-heirs with Christ!" (Romans 8:17). As an inheritance, God has given to Jesus all that He has and God has made us a joint-heir with Him. It is Jesus and what He did for us that makes us perfectly safe in Him and richly blessed!

The Gospel is good news, my friends! It is good news indeed! We are in our heavenly Goshen, Christ Jesus, and we are indeed safe and blessed! This is what God was demonstrating when He put Moses and the children of Israel in Goshen at that time. When the flies swarmed, they didn't come on them or their possessions; when locusts devoured, none of them or their belongings were consumed; and when God released a darkness so thick that the people in Egypt couldn't even see where they were going, in Goshen there was a supernatural light from God. God is doing the same for us today. "For behold, the darkness shall cover the earth and deep darkness the people, but the Lord will arise over you, and His glory shall be seen upon you (Isaiah 60:2).

Now, while the Lord had His children in Goshen safe from the judgment of God, He was also preparing them before He sent His final plague against their enemies and delivered them completely. The Lord gave His children detailed instructions of what to do with lambs, which is also represents Christ Jesus. The Lord told them that He was going to "pass through Egypt and strike the firstborn in all the land...of both man and beast; and against all the gods of Egypt

I will execute judgment" (Exodus 12:12). Thus, God instructed His children to kill and prepare an unblemished young male lamb, roast it in fire and partake of the entire lamb (Exodus 12:5-8). Then they were to take the lamb's blood and put it on the two doorposts and on the lintel of their houses. And then God promised, "when I see the blood, I will pass over you; and the plague shall not be on you to destroy you" (Exodus 12:13). Hence, the Jewish celebration of Passover was instituted.

This lamb, and the shed blood of the lamb, depicts our Lord Jesus Christ. Jesus, our true Passover Lamb, was a young male (33 years old), without blemish (without sin) when He was crucified (roasted in fire). Also, Jesus' innocent and sinless blood was shed for us at the cross so that God passes over us when His judgment is released against our enemies. This is true even when we do wrong. Remember, Moses had murdered someone, and so had Pharaoh, but when God came to execute judgment, God saw the blood on behalf of Moses, and passed over him, but as for Pharaoh, there was no blood from the Lamb atoning for his sins, and he died a horrible death. Therein lies a valuable lesson. These people were not the cause of the different outcomes they ultimately faced, and neither was their behavior. The blood of the slain lamb made the difference. Without the shedding of blood there is no remission of sins (Hebrews 9:22). And without the removal of sins there will be judgment. The children of Israel relied on the blood of the lamb, however, and the judgment of God passed over them and they were greatly blessed.

The same is true today for us believers, but so much greater because Jesus, the true Lamb of God who came down from heaven (John 1:29), has shed His blameless blood and been slain in our place at the cross, forever forgiving us all our trespasses, and making us the righteousness forevermore! Yes, the sacrifice of Jesus' life and the shedding of His blood completely surpass the blood shed in the time when Moses was alive in the earth (Hebrews 9:11-14). Moses would need to slay many more lambs in his day, but Jesus, the true Lamb of God, was crucified, and shed His blood, once for all. With Jesus' one sacrifice of Himself (Hebrews 10: 11-18), He forever removed **all** of our sins from us (Colossians 2:14), reconciled us to God forever (Romans 5:10), and made us the righteousness. Today, we don't have to anticipate any judgment from God, we just rejoice in the fact that when God passes over, He sees the blood of the Lamb shed for us and blesses us! Jesus' death and shed blood has forever made a difference between Egypt and us! Oh, what a blessed Savior we have!

The Exodus

Needless to say the Lord did it. He did what He promised. He struck the firstborn of every man and beast in Egypt, and the Bible says there had never been a cry so great as the one that came from the enemies of God that night (Exodus 11:6). Not a single child of God perished, however. And soon after this, Pharaoh realized his own son was among the dead in Egypt, his hard heart was broken, and he finally told Moses, and all of God's children, to get out of Egypt immediately! (Exodus 12:33). Notably, deliverance came suddenly for the children of God. God told me, "I am still the God of suddenly!" With that being said by God Himself, it behooves us to be prepared for the promises God made us. Although the Lord told the children of Israel beforehand when they partook of the first Passover feast that night, to eat it fast and be dressed and ready to leave Egypt as He promised, the Bible says that "they were driven out of Egypt and could not wait, *nor had they prepared* provisions for themselves" (Exodus 12:39). Even though the Lord had promised them deliverance, they were not prepared when it came. What did God teach me concerning this? The Lord told me plainly, "Faith will have you ready." Your being prepared is proof of your faith in the Lord, and what He promised to do for you. Therefore, children of God, be ready! If you are not ready, now is the time to get ready for suddenly! And because God is a God of big paybacks, be ready to come out with more than you had before. The children of Israel went from bound slaves to newfound fortune! God didn't just deliver them; He made their enemies pay them back, and caused His children to plunder their goods! The Lord made the Egyptians give His children silver, gold, clothing, and whatever else they wanted! God is the God of big paybacks! And the Lord always makes the thief pay back more than what he wrongfully took from God's people (Exodus 12:36). What has been taken from you? Peace? A loved one? Justice? Money? A relationship? Children? A marriage? Whatever it is, know, believe, and be ready for your big payback and your grand exodus because you are coming out and you will have more than before!

God Will Keep You

Remember, the Lord takes you out to bring you into the Promised Land He has for you. However, the enemy is not happy about your deliverance, and he certainly isn't thrilled that God is bringing you into abundance and blessing you so much that you will be a blessing. This demonic disposition of the devil was demonstrated by his infamous reaction to the children of Israel's deliverance on that night. After God led them out of bondage, the wicked mind of Pharaoh changed and he gathered his best army and weapons to chase down God's children, to kill them all—men, women, and children!

But God! God is not just a Deliverer, He is a keeper. God will not only bring you out and bring you out with more...He will keep you and all that He gave you. When Pharaoh caught up to the children of Israel, who were fleeing toward the red sea, they had a deep sea in front of them, and an enraged murderous enemy on their tail, but Jesus was in their midst! God parted the red sea and allowed all of His children, along with their possessions, to pass through on dry ground safely. When the enemies of God tried to pass through that same sea, however, God caused the waters to overtake them and they perished (Exodus 14:27-28). The very ditch they dug for God's children (to be killed) was the very ditch they themselves fell into (they all perished that night). That, too, is a promise from God of protection for all His children, when the enemy comes against us. The very ditch that is dug for us, God causes His enemies to fall into (Psalms 7:15-16). Not one of God's children, or their belongings, was lost! The Lord protected His children and their possessions. They didn't even drop their gold while running for their lives through the parted sea at nighttime. The revelation for us is a powerful one: God will deliver you, keep you, and keep all that He gave you. God let me know that what He gives, He surely keeps. So have no fear for yourselves, your loved ones, your possessions, or the manifested promises of God you have received. Because even if you can feel the enemy's rage against the deliverance you are experiencing, God will keep both you, and all He has given you. It is His responsibility…it is His promise to you, and it is His pleasure to give it to you (Luke 12:32).

In Closing

A lot of us have been blessed to read Exodus, and we know that God did what He promised His children who were once enslaved—but the children of Israel did not have the hindsight that you and I enjoy, at the time they were bound. They had what we have; A promise from the Lord. They had to have faith to believe that if God promised them the miracle of deliverance for them and their families, He would be faithful to do what He promised. It didn't happen overnight. It was after slavery, injustice, ten plagues, and the sacrifice and shed blood of the Passover lamb, when they were finally free! In other words, they had to let God finish! The result for them doing so is clear. God did just what He promised! And the good news for us is this: "The Lord is the same yesterday, today and forevermore" (Hebrews 13:8). So when we let God finish, He fights for us and gives us all He promised. Therefore, beloved have peace because God is fighting your battles and He is bringing you into your promised land!

"The Lord will fight for you and you shall
hold your peace." (Exodus 14:14)

CHAPTER 3:

YOU ARE REDEEMED

In Him we have redemption through His blood, the forgiveness of sins, according to the riches of His grace. (Ephesians 1:7)

WE, AS CHILDREN OF GOD, HAVE TO KNOW AND BELIEVE THIS truth: Nothing we have lost is beyond God's desire and His power to redeem. This truth remains, even if we cause the loss. Every believer is proof of this truth. Every believer has willfully sinned, and the wages of sin is death. But praise be to God, the gift of God is eternal life (Romans 6:23). Jesus not only saved our souls from hell and remitted all of our sins, but He also redeemed us from every curse of the law (Galatians 3:13). Remember the law curses when someone sins. Even though we are Christians we mess up from time to time. But because of this great sacrifice Jesus made, we are redeemed from the consequence (the curse) that comes from our willful sinning. This alone proves that God's desire is to redeem what is lost in our lives, even if the loss is because of our own doing.

Also, this redemption God provided us doesn't just include the taking away of something…the curse of the law, it provides something…an inheritance with Christ, which includes all the promises of God! For it is written, **all** the promises of God are yes and in Him (Jesus) amen to the glory of God for us believers! Now, it is important to note that God qualifies us for all His blessings the same way He removes the curse from us. He does it by His grace and not our works (Romans 4:5-8). And thus, when we flourish in morality it doesn't make God bless us, but likewise when we fail, our failure doesn't preclude us from receiving any of His blessings or promises. We see this powerful redemptive truth in the life story of Ruth by the grace God shows her and her mother-in-law despite their behavior or disqualifications. (Just note, that there are, however, consequences for our behavior, but the consequences are not God's judgment or punishment). All of our sins have already been forgiven by God and He does not even remember our sins anymore! (Isaiah 43:25). You can't punish what you don't recall. This is good news! Therefore, when we make mistakes, God isn't present to judge us. He is there to manifest the power of Jesus' redemptive work in our lives, restoring back to us what was lost. But like Ruth had to do in this beautiful life story of hers, we, too, have to let God finish!

Name Calling; A Matter of Life and Death

God told us through King Solomon, one of the wisest men to ever live, "the power of life and death is in the tongue and those who love it will eat its fruits (Proverbs 18:21). We see this truth displayed in the beginning of creation when Elohim created the heavens and the earth. God didn't get up from His throne and form and fashion the earth and everything in it; He simply opened His mouth and said what He wanted to see. For example, God said, "Light be" and light was…and light still is to this very day. Notably, when it came to God creating mankind, He said, "Let Us make man in Our image, according to Our likeness" (Genesis 1:26). And because we are made in His image and likeness, we too have creative power in our tongue. This is why we have to be mindful of what we call one another and chose our words wisely.

This powerful truth is one clearly demonstrated in the Book of Ruth. It begins with a woman named Naomi (meaning "pleasant"), her husband Elimelech, and their two sons, who they named Mahlon and Chilion. Interestingly, the name of Mahlon means, "sickly" and Chilion means, "dying" or "failing" (Nelson, NKJV Study Bible). This means that from the time these men were young, they were called "sickly" and "dying" repeatedly, day in and day out...for years. The result? Death. These two young men preceded their mother Naomi (who was a widow by that time) and their own wives in death.

A further illustration that there is indeed the power of life and death in the tongue is also given in Naomi's daughter-in-law Ruth's name. Ruth's name means "friend," and she proved to indeed be a true friend. Ruth not only honored her mother in-law while Ruth's husband was alive, but even after he died, she stuck by her side...as only a true friend would. Ruth had been called "friend" her whole life, time and time again. The result? Ruth was a friend who stuck closer than a relative. Indeed, the power of life and death is in the tongue. Thus, we should be wise in our use of words and what we call one another...even nicknames, because idle words are as powerful as intentional ones.

Therefore, husbands and wives, if there is a Godly change you want to see in your spouse, it would behoove you to say the change you desire to see, and avoid proclaiming any problems...after all, you are made in God's image and likeness. In the beginning, albeit God saw darkness and disorder, He didn't mention it once; instead He said what He wanted to see (Genesis 1). The result? What God said, was manifested! Likewise, we too can have what we say...whether good or ill, leading to life or death. Therefore, let us chose life and speak of those things that don't exist as if they did, because that is what God does.

God did this with Abraham. Abraham was about 99 years old, and his wife Sarah was about 80 years old and barren, yet God said to Abraham you are a father of many nations (Genesis 21:1-3). God didn't speak about Abraham and Sarah's age being beyond childbearing, or Sarah's womb being barren. God simply said what He wanted to see and eventually, He saw it. Sarah bore Abraham a son Isaac, even in their old age.

The same wisdom and power that God uses is available to us today. God has given us His power, shown us what to do with the power, and proven to us that it works. We would be wise to take heed of what God is showing us, learn from Him, speak what we want to see, and like God, see all that we proclaim come to pass!

Don't Run; God Blesses Beyond the Famine

At the onset of the story of Ruth, we learn something very important about God's heart toward us. God's blessings and willingness to provide for us don't depend on any circumstances around us. God is and always will be our provider (Genesis 22:14). Not understanding this produces fear, and fear often times can produce flight. In other words, someone full of fear can end up running out of the very place God ordained for them to be in, because they doubt God will provide for them there.

We see this take place in the life of Naomi and her husband Elimelech, who decided to flee their hometown of Bethlehem (which literally means, "house of bread") and go into Moab during a famine. Fear that God would not provide for them because of a famine caused them to flee the "house of "bread" and go reside in Moab (a nation previously cursed by God because of the incestuous way it began). Fear isn't rational. It caused them to leave the place called "house of bread" and take refuge in the nation that was cursed. Fear should never lead us. God promised that in His unfailing love, He will lead the people He has redeemed, and in His strength He will guide them to His holy dwelling (Exodus 15:13). Further, Jesus is our Good Shepherd, and He leads us beside the quiet waters and we shall not lack (Psalm 23:2). Notice that when the Lord leads us, we shall not lack. Now, when Naomi and her family allowed fear to lead them, they didn't lack bread in Moab, but they lacked each other, as death overtook them one by one. When God blesses you, He doesn't have to take away some blessings, in order to add more blessings to you. God is a God of multiplication, not subtraction! And if the Lord has removed something from your life, He has done it in order to give you much more! This is because our God is a giver. And this truth about God is so much so that Jesus restores that which He did not take away (Psalm 69:4).

Now, someone may be thinking this doesn't apply to them because they are not in a land that is experiencing a famine in regards to bread (i.e., food). But there may be other areas of your life where a famine seems to have hit. For example, someone may be experiencing a famine in the area of marriage. The love, intimacy, romance, and communication may seem to be in a serious state of famine, but if God is in that marriage, don't flee. Instead, believe that God will provide for you right where you are, and He will turn that famine into a feast! God is well known for blessing His people during famine. For example, God blessed Isaac right in the middle of the famine. God actually commanded that Isaac not run, but stay put because God was going to be with him and bless him right where he was. Isaac obeyed God and stayed in the land, and the Bible says that he "sowed in that land, and reaped in the same year a hundredfold; and the Lord blessed him. The man began to prosper, and continued prospering until he became very prosperous" (Genesis 26:12-13). This is our God, people!

We see God blessing His people in the middle of a famine again in the life of Joseph. During his lifetime, the Bible says that a famine arose for seven years that was "very severe." Joseph didn't run; instead He trusted God, and even though the famine was very severe, God blessed Joseph so much that he was able to open all his storehouses, which were filled with so much grain he couldn't measure it (Genesis 41:49). Beloved, it's not about the presence or absence of a famine. It is about the Lord who is with us. This is what causes us to prosper, continue prospering, and become very prosperous even in the famine! We should always remember our God is Light, and His Light is best seen in darkness. Therefore, don't flee, or be hasty, just because of darkness, but rather stand still and see the salvation of the Lord, and let His glorious Light shine so bright that everyone who sees it in your life will want the same God you have! Beloved, if you are experiencing a famine in any area of your life, know and believe that it is God's will to provide all your needs according to the riches of His grace, and to bless you to have more than enough so that you can be a blessing to others!

God Is Not to Blame

Subsequent to Naomi experiencing much tragedy and loss, she decided to go back to Bethlehem after she heard that the Lord had visited His people with bread (Ruth 1:6). Both her daughters- in-law sought to go with her to Bethlehem, but Naomi urged them not to, giving them every excuse not to follow her. She told them how she didn't have the ability to have more sons for them to marry, and went on further to discourage them from coming along by telling them even if she remarries and a miracle of childbirth occurs, they would have to wait until the child became a man. Naomi felt cursed and believed the Lord was against her. The Lord showed me something very profound from her life at this time. Naomi blamed herself for what had happened and believed that the Lord was against her. This led her to feeling cursed and worthless. God showed me how when people feel worthless, and guilty, they sabotage the good in their life because deep down they don't believe they deserve anything or anyone good. This mindset is very destructive. When people operate in this merit-mindset (you only get what you deserve), instead of God's mindset of grace (God freely gives you His blessings because you could never earn them), then they are in serious trouble. This is so because when someone believes they have to earn the goodness and blessings of God, they forfeit them. You cannot earn what God only gives freely. Naomi was operating under this merit mindset, and believed that God was against her, and therefore the tragedy she experienced was something she deserved…while the goodness of God was something she had yet to earn. The result? She did everything she could to push away the two daughters- in-law who were willing to stay by her side and help her (Ruth 1:6-7). Again, the merit-mindset is one that causes sabotage and destruction. One of her daughters-in-law turned away and didn't follow her, but the Bible says that Ruth clung to Naomi and told her "wherever you go, I will go…and your God, [will be] my God" (Ruth 1:16 Emphasis Mine). I thank God for having mercy. I say this because it was God who put His agape love in the heart of Ruth for her mother-in-law, which finally caused Naomi to receive God's help and purpose via Ruth.

Finally, Ruth and Naomi arrived in Bethlehem, and the people of the town were glad and celebrated to see Naomi, but her response to them was one saturated in condemnation and self-loathing. As they called out to her, "Is this Naomi?" she responded, "Do not call me Naomi; call me Mara, for the Almighty has dealt very bitterly with me. I went out full, and the Lord has brought me home again empty. Why do you call me Naomi, since the Lord has testified against me, and the Almighty has afflicted me?" (Ruth 1:20-21). Again, this is the fruit of Naomi's wrong thinking about God and her way to be blessed by Him. Therefore, Naomi really thought the Lord was against her and caused her tragedy and loss (Ruth 1:21). She refused to acknowledge that she and her husband made a decision apart from the Lord's direction to depart from Bethlehem and into a nation that was cursed. She refused to acknowledge that her husband and her were fearful that God would not provide for them because of a famine despite God telling His people repeatedly not to fear.

Needless to say, God was not to blame for her loss. When God showed me this, He told me and wanted me to share this with you, "Don't let need lead." God showed me this is exactly the mistake Naomi and her family made when they left Bethlehem. They had a need...there was a famine in the land, and without food the people would surely die. But God is fully aware of what we need...after all, He is the One who made us, and He is the One who made us with needs. As important as needs are, God still doesn't want need to lead us. The only One who should be leading us is God, because He will lead us correctly every time. And when it comes to our needs, God leads us concerning them through His Word spoken by Jesus Himself. Jesus addressed our needs by saying this:

Therefore I say to you, do not worry about your life, what you will eat or what you will drink; nor about your body, what you will put on. Is not life more than food and the body more than clothing? Look at the birds of the air, for they neither sow nor reap nor gather into barns; yet your heavenly Father feeds them. Are you not of more value than they? Which of you by worrying can add one cubit to his stature? So why do you worry about clothing? Consider the lilies of the field, how they grow: they neither toil nor spin; and yet I say to you that even Solomon in all his glory was not arrayed like one of these. Now if God so clothes the grass of the field, which today is, and tomorrow is thrown into the oven, *will He* not much more *clothe* you, O you of little faith? Therefore do not worry, saying, "What shall we eat?" or "What shall we drink?" or "What shall we wear?" For after all these things the Gentiles seek. For your heavenly Father knows that you need all these things. But seek first the kingdom of God and His righteousness, and all these things shall be added to you. Therefore do not worry about tomorrow, for tomorrow will worry about its own things (Matthew 6:25-34).

I am very glad that the Lord addressed these specific needs. Because if someone goes too long without eating, they will die. But even concerning the need for food, which is a matter of life and death, Jesus said then, what He is still saying to us now, "Your Father knows you have need of these things…**but seek first the Kingdom of God and His righteousness and all these things will be added to you.**" The Lord tells us what to do concerning our needs. We should mediate on God's heart of love and care for us by considering his care for birds and flowers…none of which He sent Jesus to die for, like us. He also tells us multiple times, don't worry and to seek His Kingdom and righteousness first so that all the things we need will be added to us. Notice we don't seek after provision, and instead it seeks after us. Therefore, when you seek God and His righteousness, whatever you have need of God makes it seek after you. In applying this principle, I have found that it helps to meditate on who God has made us. You are kings and priest of the Most High God. You are seated with Jesus Christ in heavenly places; and as a child of the Most High God, you have no business chasing after riches or material matters…not even food. And as a child of the Most High God, you certainly don't chase money; money chases you. You don't bow your knee to an impoverished devil in hope that he will make you rich, when your Father in heaven owns everything and has made you an heir of all that is His. Don't beg or bow for what is already yours, beloved. God has already made you an heir of His and a joint heir with Christ. The Word says that the earth is the Lord's and the fullness therein. Therefore, as an heir of God's, you possess this earth and have access via God to all that is in it. Further, the Word says that all the promises of God in Christ are yes and in Him amen. Therefore, every promise in the Word of God is your inheritance because of Christ. And it is written, I will supply all of your needs according to My riches and glory in Christ Jesus (Philippians 4:19). That promise belongs to you. Thus, if the devil tries to touch any of your needs, you can rest knowing that God is already supplying **all** of them! Also, concerning those things that we think we need, but don't have, God told me this one-day: "If you don't have it, it is because you don't need it. For I promised, 'I will supply all of your needs.'" Therefore, no matter what our circumstances say or what are emotions want to lead us to believe, if we don't have it, it is because at that moment, we don't need it! God cannot lie and He promised, "I will supply all of your needs!"

With this wisdom we can clearly see that God was not to blame for Naomi and her families loss, but their letting need lead them was. We will soon see that not only was God not to blame; He would be the only One who had both the desire and power to redeem her and her families' lives from destruction. And as we delve deeper, we will see through the life of Naomi and Ruth, Jesus' heart of love and care to provide for His people redeeming what is lost, albeit He is not to blame for the loss. Jesus indeed restores that which He did not take away.

Provision Always Precedes the Problem

Notably, as soon as Naomi and Ruth, who were two poor widows at the time, came into Bethlehem, God's provision was already there waiting for them. The Bible says that they came into Bethlehem at the beginning of barley **harvest!** (Ruth 1:22). This harvest that God provided for His people was already in full force before they arrived. God showed me this vital truth about Himself: His provision always precedes the problem. This truth is evinced throughout the life of Ruth and Naomi, as well as many others in the Bible. Not only was this truth demonstrated by them coming into Bethlehem during harvest time, it is further shown by the blessings God would later reveal to them.

Sometime after they arrived in Bethlehem, Ruth went out into the fields to do what they called gleaning. Gleaning was something that God instituted during the time of Moses as a means to provide for poor people. Those who were poor financially would go into the fields owned by rich people in order to pick up the grain that the rich left behind after they harvested their crops (Leviticus 23:22).

In those days, gleaning was something that you could say was equivalent to hitting "rock bottom" financially. But I have learned this about God: He is God at the mountaintop, and He is still God if you hit rock bottom (1 Kings 20:28). It is important for us to know and believe this truth because our financial position can fluctuate, but God remains the same. He is, and always will be, Jehovah Jireh, our Provider! Now Ruth, even at her "rock bottom" put her trust in God, believing she would find His favor while gleaning. If you are experiencing a low in any area of your life, do what Ruth did, and trust in God, because her results can be yours. The Bible says that when Ruth went out into the field to glean she, "happened to come to the part of the field belonging to Boaz, a man of **great wealth** (a relative of Elimelech, Naomi's husband) (Ruth 2:1 & 3). Now, we know that Ruth's happening to come to Boaz's field was the Lord ordering her steps (Ruth 1:16). And God being the good God that He is, ordered her steps right into this: way more provision than she ever asked or hoped for! The Bible says that when Boaz noticed Ruth in the field, he wanted to know her better. So he inquired of a servant who testified to Boaz about Ruth, saying how she came to Bethlehem with her mother-in-law, and how she had been a blessing to her (Ruth 2:11). After Boaz heard that, he went to Ruth and immediately began to bless her. He told her she was not to go into another's field to glean, but rather stay in his field by the other young women. He went on further blessing her by protecting her when he instructed the other men in the field not to touch her. He also began providing for her by telling her, if she was thirsty she could go to the vessels and draw out all the water she wanted! (Ruth 2:9). And this was just the beginning! Boaz invited Ruth to come into his house to dine with him, and she ate plenty of parched grain with vinegar and even had leftovers (Ruth 2:14). Afterwards, Boaz "commanded his young men, saying, 'Let her glean even among the sheaves, and do not reproach her. Also let grain from the bundles fall purposely for her; leave it that she may glean, and do not rebuke her" (Ruth 2:15-16). Upon leaving the field that God led her to, Ruth brought back home "about an ephah of barely" and leftovers from her favor-filled lunch with the owner of the entire field! And God still wasn't done yet. But from this provision alone, Naomi, who was once filled with bitterness and despair, cried out in joy, "Blessed be he of the Lord, who has not forsaken His kindness to the living and the dead!" (Ruth 2:20). Now, this was true about the Lord the entire time, but Naomi didn't believe until that time. Before she ever had a problem, God had Boaz, the field he owned, the great wealth He gave to Boaz and the favor and the love Ruth found with him, already in place. Naomi just had to do what we all have to do: Let God finish!

Now, Naomi's heart was open, and she began to believe in the goodness of God. Therefore, she was aligned with God's will for her life and Ruth's. With this alignment, she instructed Ruth not to go into anyone else's field to glean but to rather stay close by the other young women in Boaz's field. She also told Ruth that she wanted to seek security for her, and in so doing she received wisdom from God that changed the rest of their lives! She told her to anoint herself and go again to Boaz, who was a relative of theirs, at the threshing floor where he would be, and only after he had finished eating and drinking, lay at Boaz's feet so that he could tell her what to do. This was a marriage proposal in those days to a nearest kinsman. This was vitally important during those times, because only a nearest relative

who was willing and able could redeem a poor relative and everything that they lost due to their poverty for them. And because God
went before Ruth, He made Boaz, a man of "great wealth" a kinsman
who was both willing and able to redeem Ruth. Needless to say, Boaz
accepted the proposal, but he did so with one barrier in their way…a
closer relative was able to marry Ruth due to a Jewish law at that
time. Now, can you imagine how Ruth must have felt being on the
brink of breakthrough, just to find out a challenge stood in the way?
But Boaz reassured Ruth, like Jesus, our Redeemer, assures us whenever we face a challenge, "And now…do not fear; I will do to you
all that you require…" (Ruth 3:11). The reason Jesus can tell us not
to fear in the face of opposition is because He goes before us in any
challenge we face and His provision always precedes the problem!

We see this in the next chapter of Ruth's life. God had already
placed it in the heart of that nearest kinsman redeemer under the law
to reject Ruth's offer because she was a foreigner. God knew he would
not want a foreigner, as he risked losing his inheritance by sharing it
with a Moabites. And long before Ruth had a need to be redeemed,
God made her a Moabite…a foreigner. God knew the nearest kinsman's rejection was God's protection for these women, because Boaz
truly loved Ruth unconditionally and the other relative clearly didn't.
God is good! It is also worth noting that God shows us what to do
while waiting on God to perform the miracle we ask Him for. God
spoke through Naomi, telling Ruth what He tells us while we wait
on the Lord: "Sit still…until you know how the matter will turn out;
for the man [Jesus] will not rest until he has concluded the matter
this day" (Ruth 3:18 Emphasis Mine). In other words we can rest
while God performs His promise. When you rest, it is proof that
you trust God…it is faith in action. And we can rest, because Jesus
cares for us deeply, and He will not rest until He has given us what
we need and desire. When we rest, the Lord manifests the miracles
in our lives that we request of Him. We see this truth come alive in
Ruth's life. When she took heed to the Lord's instructions through

Naomi, Boaz redeemed Ruth and all she lost. He married her and they had a son, who became a part of the lineage of King David, the very family line Jesus Himself was born in! (Matthew 1:6). Ruth rested, and then she, who once gleaned in the field, ended up owning it! Naomi, who seemed to have lost her entire family, was being completely restored with a new family, who would be a part of the lineage of Jesus Christ, and God made her wealthy. Now, maybe to Ruth and Naomi, it initially seemed like God had forgotten them and wasn't moving in their lives. But we see the truth, and the truth is this: God was for them, and He went before them providing all they needed and desired!

Now, before we go on, the Lord wants to look deeper into the Word to see how God's provision always precedes the problem. First and most importantly, when it comes to our salvation and need for redemption, God provided this provision before the problem of sin ever arose. Let me explain. Sin came into the world when Adam and Eve disobeyed God in the Garden of Eden (Genesis 3:6). Once Adam sinned, sin came into the world and sin spread to all men because all have sinned (Romans 5:12). The wages of sin is death... (Romans 6:23). That's definitely a problem, because the Bible says, "all have sinned and come short of the glory of God" (Romans 3:23). We as humans have all sinned, and every sinner needs a savior, or they perish and go to hell. Thanks be to our gracious God, who before the foundation of the world...and long before Adam sinned in that garden, had the Lamb of God slain! (Revelation 13:8). Jesus is that Lamb and He takes away the sins of the world! (John 1:29). So you see, Jesus, God's Provision, preceded sin, a big problem! God is very good to us people! This means that before anyone prayed, fasted, touched, and agreed with each other, or used their God-given faith to believe; God provided what we needed. The good news is that God doesn't change. Now, this truth should bring you great rest. Because sometimes the enemy tries to make us feel like we have to get God to do something for us, via our prayers, faith, or even works but we see that isn't true. Before you open your mouth to speak, God has already answered you (Isaiah 65:24). The works were finished before the foundation of the world and that is why we can enter into God's rest…and receive the answer to our prayers.

Now, prayer matters, because it is communicating with God and any healthy relationship will have good communication. God wants a relationship with you. But don't allow the enemy to make you feel like God's goodness being released in your life is dependent upon your prayers or your faith, because it is not. God's everlasting love for you expressed via Jesus' finished work on the cross is the real reason God blesses us! That has already happened, and therefore we can rest and receive. God is having me share this because too often as Christians we have been told what we have to do in order for God to do for us, but God has been doing good for us even without us knowing we had a need. I truly believe God has us pray to be in fellowship with Him, and also so that when He answers, we will remember our prayer and can know that God is the one who blessed us. That way we don't give that credit to others or luck. Neither have ever given us anything. I say that respectfully, but honestly. If someone has been used by God to bless you, then know and understand that apart from Jesus they could do nothing, and therefore your help really came from the Lord. This is important to understand, because otherwise we would think our help comes from someone other than God, and this is faulty ground to be on. People change, they come and they go, and chance is as unstable as stormy waters; therefore people won't ever be able to rest if their help comes from these sources. But God is stable in all His ways, unchanging, and He remains faithful. With that kind of surety, we can rest.

To look at this truth further, see what Jesus said in John 15:5. Jesus said, "I am the vine and you are the branches. He who abides in Me, and I in him bears much fruit; for without Me you can do nothing." Although fruit hangs from a branch, which appears to have produced the wonderful fruit on it, the branch has done nothing but stay on the vine it is attached to. Likewise Jesus, the true vine, does all the work, and we His bride just stay in Him and bear much fruit that others can see in our lives. It may appear that we are very wise and successful people, but we have been made to be wise and successful by Jesus and Jesus alone. Our part is to abide in Jesus, and Jesus' part is to bear the fruit for us. In other words, God does all the work.

Lastly, it isn't just in Ruth's life where you see that God's provision precedes any problem. The Bible is filled with examples. But let's look at one of them. We see this principle clearly in the life of Elijah, the prophet. During the time of famine, God used a bird to bring food to Elijah. Eventually, that bird stopped coming (1 Kings 17:6). God knew that would happen and He had already spoke to a widow in Nahum instructing her to feed Elijah when he came to her home (1 Kings 17:8-9). God had arranged this provision before Elijah took one step in the direction of this woman's home. Provision preceded the problem in the life of Elijah, and what God did for him, and many others, He does for you!

God Remains Faithful Even if You Are Faithless

We see that God indeed blessed Naomi and her family beyond what they desired, but it is important to note the timing in which God blessed them. God didn't wait for Naomi to repent about her wrong thinking about God, and He didn't wait for her to be delivered from bitterness either; instead He blessed her in the middle of her mess. And when He did, Naomi experienced the goodness of God in such a way that it led her to repent. The Bible says it this way: The goodness of God leads to repentance (Romans 2:4). That certainly proved to be true in Naomi's life. God remained faithful to Naomi, even though she was faithless because of the hard times she had endured. Her life had undoubtedly changed, but God had not.

He loved her when she was full of faith and he loved her when she was full of bitterness. Our God is good!

Christ Revealed: Our Redeemer Lives!

There are many truths in the book of Ruth which are of importance to us as believers. However, there is a truth that is of first and most importance hidden in the life of Ruth. Jesus is the hidden heroic figure in and through Boaz. It is through Boaz that God reveals His Son Jesus as our Redeemer, who certainly lives! Jesus lives to redeem us first of all from all of our sins and every curse of the law. The Bible says it like this: "Christ redeemed us from the curse of the law, having become a curse for us—for it is written, "Cursed is everyone who hangs on a tree"—in order that in Christ Jesus the blessing of Abraham might come to the Gentiles, so that we would receive the promise of the Spirit through faith" (Galatians 3:13-14). Now, before we go further, allow me to explain to you what God taught me about the benefit of Christ redeeming His bride from the curse of the law. Before Christ shed His blood and died to remit all of our sins and rose from the dead to justify us, when someone sinned, the curse from the law came upon them, because God is a just judge. But God also loves us deeply, so when He sent Jesus to die for our sins and rose Him up from the dead for our justification, when we sin the curse from the law doesn't come upon us anymore. God literally doesn't impute our sins to us anymore, and instead imputes His righteousness to us (Romans 4:6-8). This is why there is therefore now no condemnation for those who are in Christ Jesus (Romans 8:1). So through Jesus Christ, God has made a way to bless us, in spite of the fact that we do still sin. God knew that Jesus' death specifically on a cross (a tree) would redeem us from the curse of the law. It has always been the heart of God to bless us according to the riches of His grace and not see us cursed.

Not only has Jesus remitted all our sins and redeemed us from the curse of the law, He has also made us the righteousness of God in Christ, causing us to inherit every promise of God! This is the solid foundation in which everything, worth anything, is built upon by God in our lives. Everything Jesus was smitten, died, and rose from the dead to provide for and to us, stems from Jesus as our redeemer, who has redeemed us from the consequences of our sins, and made us sons and daughters of God, and heirs of God (Romans 8:17 & Galatians 4:4-7). Jesus' perfect atonement and resurrection from the dead has made us an heir and we have all the blessings of God, less the curse of the law, although we make mistakes. Thank God for His grace!

We can see this beautiful redemption demonstrated in the book of Ruth, as Boaz, who reveals Jesus as our Redeemer, redeemed Ruth from the curse of the law and qualified her for the blessings of God by grace. Ruth was a Moabite, and just by that very fact she was under a curse from the law, and thus disqualified for the blessings of God. Likewise, when Jesus redeemed us from the curse of the law and qualified us for God's blessings, He did so by grace, and not through our works of the law. And just like there were no works Ruth could do to change who she was, a Moabite; we as believers could not do anything to change the fact that we were sinners. Thus, like Ruth, we needed a gracious Redeemer to redeem us. And because Jesus, our Redeemer, has indeed redeemed us, the Lord is saying to us, His bride, what Boaz said to Ruth: "And now, my daughter, do not fear, I will do for you all that you request" (Ruth 3:11).

Just The Way You Are!

It's not only important to know that Jesus redeemed us, but it is important to know when He did it. Also demonstrated in the book of Ruth is a picture of when Jesus redeemed us and made us His bride. Namely, when we didn't have it together at all! Boaz loved and married Ruth just the way she was, a destitute unqualified widow at her wits end. This is the way Jesus loves, weds and redeems us: just the way we are. Contrary to religious beliefs, that we must have it together in our conduct before we will be accepted and loved by Jesus, the truth is that Jesus loves us just the way we are…flaws and all. We must always remember the love of God is demonstrated toward us in this: "That while we were still sinners, Christ died for us" (Romans 5:8). In other words, when we were at our worst, God gave us His best, Jesus! God's love is unconditional and unchanging. God's love is perfect love, and perfect love is the only thing capable of casting out fear from us (1 John 4:18). Thus it is vital that we have a revelation of the love of God as revealed in the timing in which He redeemed us—while we were still in sin. If God will do the best He can do for you while you are doing the worst you can against Him, you have to know and believe that you are loved perfectly by God, and now that you have been redeemed, God won't hesitate to bless your socks off!

To further demonstrate this truth, the Word of God says, "For if when we were enemies we were reconciled to God through the death of His Son, much more having been reconciled we shall be saved by His life" (Romans 5:10). God went on further to express His unconditional love for us in the Word when the Bible says, "He who did not spare His own Son but delivered Him up for us all, how shall He not with Him also freely give us all things?" (Romans 8:32). God has already given us His best when He gave us Jesus, and in Christ is everything we could need and want. Jesus truly is the answer and God gave us Him without us praying, fasting, or following the Ten Commandments. It is important to understand this truth, because the only love you can truly find rest in, is unconditional love—the love of God. If someone believes that God loves them because of what they do, they will never be secure, because there will always be the fear that if they can't, or won't do, what it is they believe God

loves them for, then they will lose His love. God's love is unconditional and not based on you, or anything you do or don't do. God's
loves us because of who He is; and God is love (1 John 4:8). The Bible
says that God doesn't change. And because God is love, that love is
likewise unchanging! Hallelujah! When you know this truth about
God's love for you, then you will truly find rest. This is a needed
foundational rest that once achieved you can rest concerning everything else in your life. I truly believe that to the extent you have a revelation of God's unconditional and unfailing love for you, will be the
extent to which you rest. Rest is important, because when you enter
rest, you open yourself up to receive the fullness of your inheritance
in Christ. Therefore, let us believe God, and take Him at His Word,
that He loves us with an unfailing and everlasting love, just the way
we are…and He has indeed redeemed us!

> Fear not, for I have redeemed you; I have called
> you by your name; you are Mine. (Isaiah 43:1)

CHAPTER 4:

GOD GOES BEFORE YOU

And the Lord, He is the One who goes before you. He
will be with you, He will not leave you nor forsake you;
do not fear nor be dismayed. (Deuteronomy 31:6)

THE BOOK OF ESTHER IS ONE OF MY FAVORITE BOOKS TO READ
in the Bible. This was true even before God opened my eyes and
began to reveal to me powerful truths therein, which I will share
with you here. Needless to say, after the revelation was given to me I
enjoy it so much more. It has truly been a blessing to me since God's
understanding came, and I know it will do the same for you. God
began to reveal Himself and His ways as the God who goes before us
through the life of Queen Esther, and as I got to know God more, I
trusted Him more, and as a consequence I have rested more...and the
more I rested the more I received God's promises. May the same and
greater be true for you, as you see the heart of God revealed through
this life story of Queen Esther.

What God Has for You, It Is for You!

The book of Esther opens up with a man-made celebration, which quickly turns into an instigated divorce, which God ordained before the foundations of the world (Esther 1). (Now, married couples, please don't even think about filing for divorce.) I am not saying, God wants you divorced, or that God celebrates divorce in general, but I am saying God is very clear when He states, "Whatever **God joins together**, let no man tear asunder" (Mark 10:9). The doomed marriage I am referring to between King Ahasuerus and Vashti wasn't necessarily joined together by God. Thus, it was torn asunder. This needed to happen because God ordained for His daughter Esther to sit on the thrown and be married to King Ahasuerus for His divine purpose instead of Vashti. It is important to note this because when God has a purpose for you to be in a position, He will ensure that you have that place. For this reason we need not covet what someone else has, or be jealous and fearful. Whatever God determined to be yours before the foundation of the world, is yours! Esther is proof of that…and like Esther you will not have to lift a finger to make it happen. God is responsible for carrying out His will, and He is more than capable of doing so!

Many are Called; Few are Chosen

Now, after King Ahasuerus sent Vashti away for insubordination, the King had every virgin taken from their homes and brought into His palace to be given beauty treatments and preparations for an entire year in order for Him to select a new Queen from among them (Esther 2:9). Esther, a Jewish woman who was raised by her uncle Mordecai, because she was an orphan, was essentially taken by force into the king's palace, which actually was her destiny. This may seem a bit rash at first hearing, but let's be honest—sometimes being pushed or propelled into our God-given destiny is the only way some of us will go and fulfill it. You likely have heard about Jonah having that issue. Jonah was called by God to go and preach to the people in a placed called Nineveh (Jonah 1:2). As far as Jonah was concerned, Nineveh was the Sodom and Gomorrah of his day, and he wanted nothing to do with the people in that place, or his purpose for going there. Therefore, when God told him to go preach in Nineveh, so that God could use him to deliver those people from their wicked ways, Jonah fled instead (Jonah 1:3). I suppose Jonah, like many others, including myself, thought he could outrun God... who is omnipresent. (I'm trying not to laugh at Jonah...and myself.) Well, Jonah ran and went aboard a ship, which set sail in the opposite direction of where God told him to go.

But because God is omnipresent, God was right there in the boat with Jonah! A storm arose violently against the ship and everyone in it concluded that this storm was something supernatural, and was the fault of someone onboard. Jonah came forward and admitted he was the reason for their stormy season. Therefore these men tossed Jonah overboard to save their own lives, because this false refuge Jonah was hiding in (the boat) was being shaken until Jonah came out of it... and into the will of God! Oh yes, God fights for His own and for His purpose. The Lord is merciful to His own also. Therefore, God knowing that Jonah's decision to defy Him was going to lead to him being tossed overboard, prepared a great fish to swallow Jonah for his own protection (Jonah 1:17). You see, when you are God's, He is not only with you wherever you go, but He is also for you wherever you are...even in a mess of your own making! (Joshua 1:9). Before all was said and done Jonah had this revelation about God. And, it is our turn and our time to have this revelation of God's love for us too, because as humans, we won't get it right every time, even though we may want to. Therefore, it is important for us to know God is with us, and for us, no matter what! Let' settle it once and for all: God loves us unconditionally!

Now, before we move on, God showed me that despite man's free will, God's will was ultimately done in the life of Jonah and he did go preach to Nineveh like God called and chose him to do. For many this is very good news because you are praying for family members to be saved, or be delivered from certain evil bondages and fulfill their destiny, but they, like Jonah, seem to be going in the wrong direction. Don't worry, because they, like Jonah and me, do have free will, but that free will can never displace the power and wisdom of our God to get them where they need to be in this life and the next. God knows how to allow, or even create, certain circumstances that will cause the very person who has been running away from God, to have no other choice but to go fleeing where God told them to go, and to do what God called them to do! So, praying mothers and grandmothers, God is saying, you can rest! Rest knowing that the Bible says, "Many are called but few are chosen" and for those chosen by God, God will not take "no" for an answer (Matthew 22:14). When someone is chosen by God, God knows just how to allow things to happen, which will cause them to answer His call and fulfill their God-given destiny. Jonah did. He finally answered the call of God on his life, realized He was chosen, and went to preach in Nineveh. But when he did, he was just tired from running and smelling like the guts of a huge fish. So rejoice, God will save your wayward sons and daughters. Esther was kidnapped basically in order to get to where she needed to be in God. But God used even that to bless her to fulfill her destiny. I had been through a divorce, public humiliation, and one of the most tumultuous custody battles to date…before finally answering the call of God on my life, and accepting the fact that I have been chosen. The good news is, we all were chosen by God and therefore ended up going where God wanted us to go and doing what God called us to do. Thus, whether chosen people come into the will of God limping, or leaping, God's will for their life will be done, and their free will can't stop that! God will shake, or sink, whatever ship His chosen crawl into to hide! So what shall all the chosen of God say to all these things? "I will see you in Nineveh!"

Now, for Esther, it may have seemed like she was just taken away because of the king's command, but the reality was God had a plan for her life and it included her being inside the kingdom. This truth is evidenced by the fact that the king had his officials gather every beautiful young virgins from that entire province, but was only selecting one woman to be queen (Esther 2). The Bible says, "Esther obtained favor in the sight of all who saw her," and when it was her turn to go into the king's royal palace, "[the king] loved Esther more than all the other women, and she obtained grace and favor in his sight more than all the virgins" (Esther 2:15 & 17). God clearly ordained Esther to have favor for His purpose. He also made Esther a woman of worth. The Bible says this about women of worth: "many have done well, but you excel them all" (Proverbs 31:29). And indeed, there were many young beautiful virgins brought before the king, however, Esther excelled every woman around her, because the king "set the royal crown upon her head and made her queen" (Esther 2:17).

Fear Not, God Draws the Enemy Out!

After Esther had been made queen, all seemed to go well. There was a great feast the king made, the Feast of Esther, to celebrate that wonderful time (Esther 2:18). However, afterwards, Mordecai, the uncle of Queen Esther, was sitting outside the king's gate and overheard the king's eunuchs, Bigthan and Teresh, plotting to murder the king (Esther 2:21). Mordecai told Queen Esther, who informed the king, which resulted in saving the king's life. Both of the conspiring eunuchs were hung on gallows for their treason, and a record of it was written in the book of the chronicles (Esther 2:23). We can see the difference now between a God-given wife (Queen Esther, who was instrumental in saving the life of her husband), and a wife a man chooses for himself (Vashti, who broke her own husband's laws, thereby risking a rebellion in the entire kingdom). Needless to say, it is better to let God choose!

After the execution, the king promoted Haman, who was an enemy of the Jews, and advanced him and set his seat above all the princes and all the king's servants. Keep in mind that the king didn't know that Haman hated the Jews, or that his wife Esther was a Jew... Mordecai had instructed her not to tell anyone she was Jewish. We will see that the decision to keep her Jewish decent a secret was not from Mordecai, but was the wisdom of God Himself. Because of Haman's high-level position in the kingdom, the king commanded that all the king's servants who were inside the king's gate had to bow down to Haman to pay homage. Mordecai was one such person, but he refused to bow to that hateful man. Haman, who was already filled with pride, became filled with wrath when someone told him that Mordecai refused to bow to him. In fact, he became so enraged that he disdained to just kill Mordecai and instead sought to murder every Jewish person in the king's entire province! (Esther 3:6). This man was definitely proud. It didn't matter to him one bit, nor was it nearly enough, that everyone else bowed to him; he just had to have Mordecai's worship, too. Thank God, because it is surely written that pride comes before destruction (Proverbs 16:18).

Now, this murderous madman didn't have the authority to destroy his enemies, as he desired. Therefore, Haman manipulated the king, convincing him to use his authority to carry out Haman's wicked agenda. Let the leaders beware! A wise leader will do like Solomon did, and pray for God's wisdom in order to judge righteously. This can prevent abuses of their God-given authority. Now, that principle is true in general, but in this instance, God wanted

Haman to do this, not to harm His people, but that Haman's heart would finally be exposed. The king issued a death-decree at the direction of Haman to destroy, kill, and annihilate all the Jews, both young and old, little children and women, in one day, on the thirteenth day of the twelfth month...the month of Adar. And as if that wasn't enough, the decree ordered that the Jews' possessions be plundered too (Esther 3:13).

Thereafter, Mordecai and the other Jews within the king's province became aware of the king's decree. During those days, there was no court of appeals. Once a king issued a decree, it could not be overturned, not even by the king who issued it (Esther 8:8). I'm pretty sure the Jewish people of that day felt that their fate was sealed. They were in great mourning, fasting, weeping, and wailing while dressed in sackcloth and ashes. Mordecai too, was in anguish, crying out in public with a loud and bitter cry, even as far as the king's gate (Esther 4:1-2). I can understand their reaction. They had a vast-approaching death sentence, which could not legally be reversed. There was nothing they could do to save themselves. They had no choice but to let God finish what He began in their lives.

When Esther was made aware, she too, was deeply distressed and sent her servants to make contact with her uncle Mordecai. This is when God revealed to Mordecai Esther's purpose in being made queen. He charged Esther to go before the king and "plead before him for her people" (Esther 4:8). Esther, however, like some others who realize what God has called them to do, was afraid and unwilling to embrace her destiny. Moses made every excuse he could not to do what God called him to do. Jonah initially would rather camp out in the guts of a fish before he answered the call of God on his life. I too made every excuse not to do what God called me to do, until every excuse was literally removed from my life! Mordecai, unmoved by Esther's fear and hesitation, both admonished and encouraged her; telling her that if she thought she would escape death because she was inside the king's palace, she was wrong. In other words, she was a Jew whether in the palace or outside on the porch, and the decree issued ordered all Jews (no matter their location) to be destroyed, killed and annihilated (Esther 3:13). He encouraged her by pointing out her God-given purpose and destiny to her...telling her; perhaps you have come to the kingdom for such a time as this (Esther 4:14). In other words God made you Queen and gave you that marriage for His purpose and not just you and your spouses enjoyment. (I'm sure God is speaking to someone married right now).

It seemed like once Esther heard that encouragement; she was willing to go before the king in order to do the will of God. Esther instructed all the Jews to gather together and fast for her before she went, because the law in that country was such that if anyone went before the king uninvited, the penalty was death, except for the one whom the king chooses to extend his scepter. Now, understand Esther's point of view; at this time she had not called by her husband to come into his chambers for thirty days! Esther probably didn't know if she was on the verge of a divorce, let alone whether she had enough favor with her husband to come before him and blatantly break his law but circumvent death. I'm sure the devil was telling her, "you remember what happened to his last wife, who broke his law...you are for sure going to die, if you go before the king." God has exposed this tactic of the devil to me...he is always trying to paralyze someone with fear, so they don't go forward and fulfill their destiny. God has taught me; the devil has no power at all against you and cannot stop you from fulfilling your destiny, because if he could, he would just do it. But since he absolutely cannot, he tries to get you to do it...because God has given you power...in fact God has given His children all power and authority over the enemy! (Luke 10:19).

But Esther, in the face of insurmountable odds, and lies from the enemy, did what we all have to do in order to fulfill our God-given purpose in life: She loved not her life, even unto death. This is what Jesus Himself had to do too. Esther said in her heart and out of her mouth "I will go before the king, which is against the law; and if

I perish, I perish!" (Esther 4:16). This seems like weakness and giving up, but for God it is not. It is a sign of the greatest strength. It is humility at its best, and God always exalts the humble (1 Peter 5:6).

Well, after three days of fasting and praying, the time came for Esther to go before the king…and after spending that time with God; she was well prepared, and filled with wisdom, grace and favor from God! Whoever God calls, He equips! (Hebrews 13:20-21). Esther was equipped with wisdom so she didn't go before the king and immediately begin exposing Haman and telling the king her problems; she went and asked if he didn't mind that she would like to honor him (and Haman) with a feast she prepared. This is a wise woman! And, Haman, blinded by pride, went out from the palace that day more secure than ever that he was in good graces with the royal family. His false sense of joy quickly vanished, however, the moment he saw Mordecai outside still refusing to bow to him. That is when Haman reared more of his ugly head and heart. He went home boasting to his wife and friends about being invited to Queen Esther's banquet, yet venting about his inability to enjoy life because one Jew refused to bow to him (Esther 3:2). Again, pride always comes before destruction. Haman's wife and friends suggested that he have a fifty-cubit-high gallow built and go out to the king in the morning to suggest that Mordecai be hung on it (Esther 5:14). But God!

That same night, God refused to allow the king to sleep and gave the idea that the book of their kingdom's records be read to the king to help him get rest (Esther 6:1). And God caused the reader to read aloud to the king how Mordecai had told of Bigthana and Teresh's plot to murder the king. At that moment, King Ahasuerus realized nothing had been done for Mordecai, who had saved the king's life! (Esther 6:2-4). Now, for some, Mordecai's honor was late, but God is always on time. It had surely been some time since Mordecai discovered that plot against the king and the king had not so much as said thanks. But even that delay of thanksgiving was the will of a loving God. If God would have had Mordecai honored prior to this time, Haman never would have blatantly confessed his hate for the Jews and been a hidden enemy right in their midst with the ability to kill them without them even knowing. God knew this, so in His infinite wisdom He allowed what seemed like a delay of honor. If you have been overlooked and under-honored, just know that God still has a plan for you, and it is for your good. It certainly was for Mordecai and the Jews of that day, and God is not a respecter of persons. And we can see that God is always on time. Mordecai was going to be hung that very next morning…but God, who goes before us, went before Mordecai and kept the king up at night to hear and remember what Mordecai had done for him. Again, God is always on time!

Now, Haman, who was too late because God was not for him, came into the king's palace early the next morning prepared to ask that Mordecai be hung on the gallows he built, but before the words could come out of his mouth, the king asked him what should be done for a man the king delights to honor? And arrogant Haman just knew the king was talking about him, so he suggested that "a royal robe be brought which the king has worn, and a horse on which the king has ridden, which has a royal crest placed on its head. Then let this robe and horse be delivered to the hand of one of the king's most noble princes, that he may array the man whom the king delights to honor (Esther 6:8-9). Pride is blinding!

When the king informed Haman that it was Mordecai whom the king wanted to honor, he then instructed Haman to "Hurry, take the robe and the horse, as you have suggested, and do so for Mordecai the Jew who sits within the king's gate" (Esther 6:10). And Haman having no choice but to obey the king's command, took the robe and the horse, arrayed Mordecai, and led him on horseback through the city square, and proclaimed before him, 'Thus shall it be done to the man whom the king delights to honor!' (Esther 6:11). Yes, God has a sense of humor!!! (Psalms 2:4 & 37:13). That is hilarious! Every time I read it, I laugh!

Now, Esther still operating in God's wisdom held the first banquet, but held her tongue to disclose to the king the problem with Haman and instead invited them to a second feast. Well the time came for the second banquet, which Esther prepared for the king and Haman, and having used the wisdom God gave her, she finally disclosed to the king what Haman had done. Esther didn't ask the king to kill or even harm Haman for what he had done, she asked that her life, and the life of her people, be spared, and explained to the king that the enemy could never compensate him for the loss of his wife. Oh, the riches of the wisdom of our God! Esther didn't make it about her people and Haman; she made it about Haman the King. Needless to say, the king was furious! Now, Haman, the same man who caused a whole nation of people to fear, was so freaked out in fear himself that he fell on the lap of the queen pleading for his life. When the king saw it, he didn't see a desperate man in fear of dying, he saw Haman assaulting his wife. Haman had lost all favor he ever had with the king. The king ordered that Haman be killed…with no trial, no lawyer or opportunity to present any evidence! Haman received the very judgment he wanted for Mordecai, the child of God. And I do mean the very thing, because the king ordered that Haman be hung on the same gallows that he built for Mordecai! (Esther 7:10).

God showed me something very important that He wants me to share with you all from this life story. It was God who drew Haman out. God draws the enemy out, and although that can be scary at times, God has a purpose in doing so, and that purpose is for the good of His children. Haman was among those Jewish people with that murderous hate in his heart the whole time, and God's people had a deadly enemy among them, which they weren't even aware of. That's very dangerous, so God drew Haman out. God did not draw him out to destroy His people, but to expose him as their enemy, so that he would be taken down once and for all. God allowed Haman, as He does our enemies, to lift up his evil head against the people of God, so that when he lifts it up, God cuts it off! And when God does this; the enemies we once saw, we see again no more (Exodus 14:13). Therefore, do not fear if God has drawn out your enemies. It is for their destruction, not yours. God revealed this to David, as seen in Psalm 37. David said, "I have seen the wicked in great power [a rising up]," and he also says, "for they shall soon be cut down like the grass" (Psalm 37:2). That grass must come up in order to be cut down! God also demonstrates this with Pharaoh. The Bible says God hardened Pharaoh's heart and it was God who provoked Pharaoh to pursue His people…not to frighten them, but so that God would destroy their enemy once and for all (Exodus 9:12). Thus, if your enemy has lifted up his head against you, child of God, know and believe that God draws the enemy out like bait to a fish, to deal with the enemy once and for all in your life!

Lastly, if anyone is thinking that judgment from God against His enemies sounds a bit harsh, I don't think you've thought it through. Haman was an Amalekite. This was a people who the Lord instructed King Saul many years prior to destroy while at war with them. King Saul refused to obey God and left them alive. One of the decedents of those people was Haman. Haman was willing to kill every man, woman, and innocent child…just because they were Jewish. Not only that, his murderous rampage would have essentially cut off the blood line of Jesus Christ, who God ordained to be born as a Jewish man. Thus, Haman's evil sought to have us without our Savior Jesus, which would have had us all dead and in hell. Therefore, we can see that God's judgment against that wicked man was both just and necessary. It was for Christ's sake…and ours.

Provision Always Precedes the Problem

Lets expound a bit more on what God taught us: "Provision always precedes the problem," I want to share with you how God, sometimes conceals this promised provision and why. It is not so that we panic, but that the enemy will not see his downfall until it is absolutely too late for him to do anything about it. We, as God's children, are called by God to walk by faith and not by sight, which means even if you don't see the provision, know and believe, that it has preceded any problem you face. We can see this in the life of Esther. Her enemy, Haman, had been promoted to a high-level position of authority, had a relationship with the king that was such that when Haman asked the king to issue a decree he wanted, the king took off his ring of authority and handed it over to Haman to do whatever he desired! That was a problem for Esther and her people. What Esther and her kinsman did not see, was that God had already sent the provision before that problem arose. Long before Haman was promoted, God had already strategically placed Esther inside the kingdom, made her queen, and gave her both grace and favor with the king, so much so that he "loved her more than all the other women." Not only that, but long before Haman issued that death decree against His people, God placed Mordecai outside the king's gate where he alone overheard a plot to kill the king, and reported it to Esther, which saved the life of the king! Now, it's one thing to do something nice for the king and be in his good graces; it is wholly different to save his life! This caused this king to be indebted to Mordecai to the extent of his very own life. Haman may have had some temporal favor with the king (for whatever is done of the flesh or the devil is temporary), but God gave Mordecai powerful favor that lasted. And the wisdom of our God didn't allow the favor to manifest until it was the appointed time. Again, if God would have had the king honor His son Mordecai sooner, Haman would have known not to attack the Jews in an obvious manner; but because his heart was filled with hate for them, he would have still attacked them, just in a more cunning and subtle fashion. The way God dealt with their problem was with wisdom. He drew out the hate in Haman's heart (again not to terrify His children, but that their enemy would be revealed and destroyed), and by the time Haman realized that revealing the hate in his heart was to his own demise...it was too late! Haman could not cover up or conceal what God allowed to already be exposed!

God also showed me He is an on-time God with His provision. Haman had prepared to kill Mordecai early in the morning and already had the gallows built which he wanted to hang Mordecai on. But God, preceded that problem, Haman's evil plan, with a divine plan of His own, having already had Mordecai discover the plot against the king, reveal it to the king via Esther, and had it recorded in the book of the Chronicles...God knowing that He would cause that king to not sleep and the account of Mordecai saving his life would be read to him, just in time to save Mordecai's life! It was hours before Mordecai was to be hung, that God finished this miracle—which was on time. We serve and on-time God!

This has happened in my own life. I remember I had a very important court hearing coming up the next morning and I had a vital decision to make beforehand. I had no idea what to do and with every passing minute, I felt more afraid, because I didn't have an answer from God. When I went to sleep (a state whereby I was not anxious and fearful, but rested), God spoke to me in a dream and gave me the answer. I arose from the dream at about 4:00 AM (court was at 9:00 AM that morning) and I texted my lawyer the answer. But there was still something I was unsure about. I went back to sleep, and God showed me in a dream that if I go in a certain legal direction, the exact result it would cause, and it was of terrible consequence. I arose from that dream, and it was about 7:00 AM, and I texted my lawyer again and gave more clear direction to her. She went to court with God-given directions and I escaped completely safe from the plans of the enemy, which were very contrary to me! God is good, and God is on time!

Not only did God show me how His provision proceeded Esther and Mordecai's problems as described above, He told me, He went before His people providing for them by having Vashti removed from the throne in order for Esther to occupy it. When that occurred the Jews had no idea that they had a fierce enemy among them, who hated them so much he would kill them and their innocent children. But God knew, and so before the Jews could pray, plead, fast, or cry, God had already begun to answer them. This is what God means when He promises, "Before you open your mouth to speak, I have already answered you" (Isaiah 65:24). God's provision most certainly **always** precedes the problem!

Don't Bow

Remember, Haman became exceedingly wrathful and hateful when Mordecai refused to bow to him. This God showed me was not a unique experience belonging to Haman. This is something that the enemy tries to do to every child of God—get them to bow. But God said, "Don't bow!" God made you the head, and not the tail, **above only** and not beneath! (Deuteronomy 28:13). Therefore, don't you dare bow to a defeated devil, who has been stripped of any power at all against you (Colossians 2:15). God put you in a position of authority and granted you His power so don't cower to that fearful serpent. The temptation to bow for Mordecai is symbolic of what the enemy tries to get us to do today in various ways. God showed me two ways this attack comes, one specifically assigned against women and the other men.

Ladies first, so let's begin with how the enemy tries to get women to bow to him. God showed me the enemy almost always attacks a woman's worth. The devil tries desperately to get them to believe his lie that because they don't look a certain way, they don't measure up…to his standard of worth. However, women: Your worth has nothing to do with your looks. God called His daughters women of worth and whatever God says is the truth and cannot be undone. In Proverbs 31 when God speaks about a woman of worth, He addressed looks and appearances in relation to a woman's worth.

God said, "Charm is deceitful and *beauty is fleeting*, but a woman who fears the Lord (A Woman of Worth), she shall be praised! Give her the fruit of her hands and let her own works praise her in the gates!" (Proverbs 31:30). In other words God gives no credence to a woman's looks in reference to her worth. Women, it is God alone who made you, and Jesus who bled and died for you, because that is how much Jesus has determined you are worth! Don't believe anything less than that, because that is the truth.

Also, God wants you to know that your worth far exceeds any amount of money any man could ever give you. The Son of God left heaven and all its glory and splendor to be beaten to the point that He was disfigured and marred, spat on, mocked, humiliated, falsely accused, falsely imprisoned, wrongfully convicted, bled, and died destitute and naked other than the crown of thorns which crushed his skull, only to go straight to hell afterward…and all for you!!! Women of God, you have so much worth that it cannot be measured, and it certainly cannot be bought. You are not for sale. It doesn't matter how rich he is because; with all the money in the entire world, he still CANNOT afford you! Again, you are not for sale. Don't dare bow, by putting up with the devil through a man who abuses you whether emotionally, physically, sexually, or in any other manner, when you are a Queen called and created by God! Jesus wore a crown of thorns and suffered humiliation so that you could wear His crown of honor, favor, and glory, less the humiliation. Don't bow to the enemy or anyone else, by believing or accepting less than the truth about who you are and what you are worth. You are and always will be who God says you are. And God says, you are A Woman of Worth!!! This worth is far above rubies (money). Therefore, women of worth don't dare bow in your character of Christ for a man or his money. Your worth can never be bought and your worth isn't for sale!

Men, God wants to tell you the truth about your worth: Your self-worth is separate and apart from your net-worth! You are who God called you to be and that is a king and a priest. This is your identity! You are nothing less than God's very best and you are made in the very same image as God, and God is perfect! Therefore, so are you! This doesn't change with your salary or depend upon what accolades you possess or whether according to this world you have accomplished what they think you should have. Don't bow to this foolishness. You are who God says you are! You are fearfully and wonderfully made (Psalm 139:14). That is the truth about you. Society cannot tell you what a man is supposed to look like or have, because society didn't make you; God did. God made man. God alone, as your Creator, knows what you are and what you are worth. The world is lost. Don't look to the lost to tell you what you are worth. Don't look to famous rappers either, with rented cars and rented women on music videos, to tell you that this is what you should have in order to be a man. That's not what makes you a man. When God created the first man (Adam), God made him to rule over all other creation. Cars, money, and every material possession was created by God for men to rule over, not to rule over men. Men, don't you dare bow to money. That is the one thing that God has stated affirmatively will completely prevent a man from loving and serving God. God said, "No one can serve two masters; for you will hate the one and love the other, or else he will be loyal to the one and despise the other. You cannot serve God and mammon (*money*)" (Matthew 6:24 Emphasis Mine). Don't you dare go to hell, or even have a life of pain and disappointment, for putting money in a place it doesn't belong…a place superior to you! You are worth more than all the money in the entire world. You need to know and understand that Jesus has died a horrible death and went all the way to hell because you are worth so much to Him that He would rather die and go to hell than to have you go through it. Men, your worth far exceeds money and material possessions. And if someone cannot see that truth about you, they just simply don't have a revelation yet, but their ignorance doesn't make you worthless.

And men, don't dare bow to money for a woman's sake...thinking that that is what a woman wants. That is a lie. That may be what a prostitute wants, but a woman of worth wants a man after God's own heart! I am a woman who God has blessed with some wealth and God has placed me in relationships with women who are rich. I know a lot of them, and I am telling you that these women who have had men with a lot of money were depressed, abused, feeling worthless, cheated on, lied to, or worse! Nearly every one of these women had an affair with a "poor man." That should tell you a lot!!! And as for me personally, I will tell you this: I was once married to a "rich man" and I divorced him! It was only when he was rich in a certain character reflecting Christ...and without money, that I married him! A real woman of worth wants to be loved and give love; she doesn't want your money and won't make you feel less than who you are whether you have money or not! She won't be depending on you as the supply for her needs; she knows God supplies all of her needs and yours. She won't be in your life for money; she will be there because God sent her.

People who go after the riches of this world instead of going after God may make some money, but it will enslave and bind them, and they will soon will be miserable! That is not wealth. True riches are the things that money cannot buy—for example (and this is not an exhaustive list), a relationship with God, love, wisdom, peace of mind, a good spouse, health, and long life.

Men, you were never meant to waste your years or nullify your relationship with God, for money. Jesus has a God-ordained way for you to be wealthy. Jesus said, "Seek first the kingdom of God and His righteousness and all these things will be **added to you**" (Matthew 6:33). Notice that God said all these things will be added to you. True wealth from God seeks after you while you seek after God. Don't go after money; go after God, and God will make money go after you for God's purpose and your good and the good of others. This will make you truly rich and no sorrow will be added to it (Proverbs

10:22). And as a man God made, you deserve nothing less than God's best, because that is what Jesus died to give you. Don't reject the greatest gift from God; His Son Jesus and all He died and was resurrected to give you. The Bible says that Jesus became poor that through His poverty, you would become rich. God has a way to supply your needs, over and above what you ask or think, so don't bow to the enemy. I am telling you—and more importantly God Himself is promising you—that you are worth more than that!

Therefore, men and women of God, let us, like Mordecai, refuse to bow to the enemy…no matter how furious he gets, what threats he makes, or what pressure he applies. Let us refuse to accept anything less than the truth. We are who God says we are, and we are men and women of immeasurable worth! This worth is separate and apart from our net worth or our physical appearance. We are, and always will be, who God says we are, and God alone determines our great value!

Beauty for Ashes

One of the things that God called Jesus to do for us was to turn our ashes into beauty (Isaiah 61:3). In other words, Jesus turns evil into good for us. There is a picture of the Lord's heart to do this for us is demonstrated in the book of Esther too. Although Haman had been killed and the evil intentions of his heart exposed, the decree he had issued against the Jews was still outstanding, because pursuant to the Persian laws of that day, it had to be executed once issued. But God in His love and mercy for His people, gave them wisdom again, and had them issue a counter-decree, which ultimately delivered them from this so-called set-in-stone death decree. Since God had already strategically placed Esther into the kingdom, she too had authority and power in Persia as the Queen. The king asked Esther what would she like to decree, and Esther, full of wisdom, used her

God-given authority to issue a counter-decree that allowed the Jews to defend themselves, Haman's sons to be hung, and his house to be given to Mordecai (Esther 7:10; 8:2). We, as children of the Most High God, must do the same, and use our God-given authority. Now, I know that someone may be saying, "but I'm not a queen and I don't have the authority to issue court decrees like Esther." But indeed you are a queen, and for the gentlemen reading, you are a king in the eyes of God, and you have God-given authority to issue decrees in the highest court of heaven. The Bible says that He made us kings and priests and Jesus has given us His keys to the Kingdom, and we have all power and authority over the enemy. Therefore, your authority is even greater than Esther's was in that day, and Esther was used to save an entire nation! Therefore, with the wisdom of God, use your God-given authority, because we—like Esther—have authority with the King!

So after the counter-decree was issued, it happened that on the same day that the children of God were supposed to die, their enemies perished instead. During the month that they were supposed to be unjustly slain, God gave them rest from their enemies…turned their sorrow to joy, and they went from mourning to a holiday (the Feast of Purim, which commemorates this victory) (Esther 9). And to this day many Jews still celebrate the Feast of Purim with feasting, gladness, and sending one another gifts, because of the greatness of our God and what He did in Persia. The Lord is willing and able to do the same for you. Whatever was meant for your harm, God works it together for your good. And remember; don't be afraid of any weapon that forms against you because it will never prosper. And know that if God allowed the weapon to form, God can take that very same weapon and wield it against your enemy. The Bible says that the pit that the enemy digs for you, he himself will fall into (Proverbs 26:27). That is what God did for Mordecai. God allowed his enemy Haman to build the gallows, thinking it was for Mordecai. The truth was, God knew Haman would hang on that very same gallows in his stead! And, God changes not! What

He did for them, He will do for you. Therefore, don't be afraid when you see your enemies digging ditches, because they are digging their own graves and whatever ashes they threw your way, Jesus will give you beauty in place of it!

We Need You

The Bible says that Mordecai said to Esther, when she was charged with going before the king to plead for the life of her people, "perhaps you have come into the kingdom for such a time as this" (Esther 4:14). Perhaps you, like Esther, have come into the Kingdom of God for such a time as this, and your people (your brothers and sisters in Christ) need you and what God put inside you, like the Jews needed Esther. God created you for a purpose and He has imparted gifts inside of you for His divine purpose. God used Esther, a female orphan, to save an entire nation! Being an orphan likely carried with it a hardship, but on top of that she was a female in a foreign land. That complicated matters. Women were not treated equally, and then as a Jew in a foreign land let's just say she had more than enough odds stacked against her. But regardless of the opposition, God created Esther with a divine purpose, as He has created you with a divine purpose as well. And just as significant as Esther's purpose was significant, so is yours. You, as a member of the body of Christ, are vital to the rest of the body and this lost world. Just as each part of a natural body has essential functions, even more so does every part of Christ's body. No part of the body of Jesus Himself is insignificant, and neither is one part more important than the other. You, and your God-given purpose, are important to God, to His body, to the lost souls in this world…and to me.

And please don't think that by you being one person, you can't do much anyway. The Bible says, that by one man (Adam), all were made sinners (Romans 5:19). Adam did one thing that changed the entire condition of humanity. Praise be to God that also by One man's obedience (Jesus), many will be made righteous (Romans 5:19). Jesus' one sacrifice has changed the condition of many for all of eternity! You and your individual purpose are significant. We need you, and you need to know that. Allow God to fulfill your purpose through you for all our sakes. And be unafraid to ask God what that purpose is and to help you fulfill it, because Jesus is both able and willing to reveal it to you and help you accomplish it!

Marriage with a Divine Purpose

Before concluding, I want to share with you something God revealed to me specifically for the married while studying the book of Esther. Esther and the king's marriage had a much greater purpose than two people who just loved one other. That's the truth about God's marriages (i.e., those men and women who He joins together). We need to remember this when tempted to walk away...God has a purpose for your marriage beyond yourself, your emotions, and even your rights. I say this because you may be right regarding a problem that arose in your marriage, but please keep in mind that when your marriage serves a greater purpose—one beyond your-self—others can be gravely affected by your decision to exercise "your right." Let us always remember, being right isn't enough. We have to remain unselfish. Love doesn't seek its own even when it is right. (1 Corinthians 13:4-5). We know this is true by looking at Jesus. Jesus did no sin, knew no sin, and in Him was no sin, but the sin of the entire world came upon Him at the cross for a greater purpose, and Jesus allowed it to be so that through His sacrifice, this entire world can be saved forever (John 3:16-17). Jesus gave up His right to be right, and chose love and humility instead. I say humil-ity, because although Jesus had not committed the crimes He was falsely accused of, and certainly was not subject to the death penalty,

He—being God—subjected Himself to the governing authorities of man, in order to do the will of God. The Bible says, "He humbled Himself and became obedient to the point of death" (Philippians 2:18). Sometimes in a marriage the only thing that needs to be done in order to be humble is to close our mouths, even if we are right. By the grace of God, we can do this. The Bible says, "we can do all things through Christ who strengthens us" (Philippians 4:13).

Now, keep in mind that Jesus gave up His right to be right because of love. And Jesus, who certainly knows how to defend, as seen throughout the entire Bible, refused to defend Himself when His life was on the line. Instead, He remained silent, renouncing all rights He had as God, and as an innocent Man, so that we, who caused His death, would be completely forgiven and made righteous by God forever. This is LOVE! Love is completely unselfish; it truly does not seek its own. Again, being right isn't what matters; love does. I'm not saying that this is so easy to do all the time, especially with the flesh, but it is necessary in marriage.

Also, when you have a God-ordained marriage, your marriage is a ministry...and the world benefits from it. It is in all of our interest that your marriage remains together and strong...and it is to our detriment if it doesn't. Please remember God, and us, whenever a trial comes; because your marriage isn't just about you and your spouse. Also, keep in mind that whatever problem has arisen, it is passing. It is not in your marriage and life to stay. Just know, this too shall pass. But the God-ordained purpose for which your marriage serves is eternal and will have eternal consequences for the glory of God and the good of multitudes of God's people.

Also, please keep this in mind: God said, "For everyone to whom much is given, from him much will be required; and to whom much has been committed, of him they will ask the more" (Luke 12:48). Your marriage has a divine purpose and that means much has been given you. Humbling ourselves and walking in love is the much that is required from God. And, for those facing a storm right now, do not think, and definitely don't believe and confess, that "I cannot take or make it," because those are lies! God has promised, and He cannot lie, that "My grace is sufficient for you" (2 Corinthians 12:9). You can make it! And don't be discouraged if your spouse isn't praying with you for your marriage. You and God are a majority! Esther's husband never prayed with her during the storm she faced; in fact, he was completely oblivious that his marriage was about to end and his own wife would be killed. Esther had a relationship with God, and she cried out to God, without her husband even being aware of her prayer, let alone participating in it; and indeed that was more than enough! It saved her, her people, and her marriage. God is not a respecter of persons; if He did it for Esther (and we know He did), He will do it for you!

God's Heart Revealed

Before closing this chapter, I want to share with you some truths about the heart of God for us that are revealed in the book of Esther. These truths will certainly bless your life! King Ahasuerus in the book represents God. Esther, the bride, symbolizes the church (Christians). The first decree issued against the children of God, demanding their death, represents the law (the first covenant). God calls the first covenant (the law) given through Moses, a ministry of death (2 Corinthians 3:9). The last decree issued, which saved the children of God, represents the New Covenant, which Jesus Christ provided for us by His grace. When Esther went before the king un-summoned to ask that the lives of the Jews be spared, King Ahasuerus held out a golden scepter, which Esther had to touch. We learn in Hebrews 1:8 that God's scepter is a scepter of righteousness. And in Romans 1:17, we learn that "the righteousness of God is revealed from faith to faith; as it is written, "The just shall live by faith." Again, Esther represents for us the bride of Christ, and the king represents God. Thus when the bride of Christ reaches out to receive the freely extended grace and righteousness of our God, our lives are spared and the handwriting that was contrary to us, Jesus wipes out! Hallelujah!

In Closing

Always, remember this truth about God, as reflected in the life story of Esther: God goes before you. God had already began to help His children long before they even realized they needed His help... and God knew the trouble they were facing well before they were enlightened. God had gone before them already. And albeit, this was true, the Jews of that day still had to do, what we must all do as children of God: We have to let God finish! And when we let God finish as they did, we too will have any mourning turned into holidays and celebrations!

Weeping may endure for a night, but joy
comes in the morning. (Psalm 30:5)

CHAPTER 5:

FOR GOD'S GLORY!

I am the Lord, that is My name; and My glory
I will not give to another. (Isaiah 42:8)

MANY ARE ASKING THE LORD WITH SINCERE HEARTS, questions like, Lord why haven't you delivered me, or delivered my loved one? Or, why Lord are you allowing it to go from bad to worse? Don't You see, Jesus, what I am going through, and that I am ready to give up? Lord, don't You hear my cry? The Lord has sent me to tell you that He has heard your cry, He has seen your tears, and He will deliver you (2 Kings 20:5). The Lord has also sent me by His Spirit to answer these legitimate questions that His children have, and provide understanding. God promised, happy is the man who has understanding (Proverbs 3:13). So get ready to be happy, free from despair, and completely delivered!

You Are Who God Says You Are!

When the Lord began to minister to me about the questions He's being asked, He led me to the book of Daniel in the Bible, and had me to look at the life of three Jewish boys, in order to provide answers to these important questions.

Shadrach, Meshach, and Abed-Nego were the newly given names of these three boys, who all loved and served God faithfully. After being exiled out of their own land and driven by force into the land of Babylon, they were mandated to serve the conquering king Nebuchadnezzar...who by no means was a believer in God. Immediately, under his wicked rule, he began trying to change everything that meant anything about these three boys. He forced them to learn his language, literature, customs, and foreign ways... all of which were not the ways of God. He also changed their names. He changed the name of one from Hananiah (meaning "the Lord is gracious") to Shadrach (meaning "I am fearful of the God"), and Mishel (meaning "who is what God is") to Meshach (meaning "I am of little account"), and lastly, Azariah (which means "the Lord has helped me") to Abed-Nego (which means "servant of the god [Nebo]," who was a false god of the Babylonians) (Daniel 1:6-7). Of all the changes that this king implemented, the changing of their names may have had the most significant effect. For God, names are very significant. Additionally, a person's name is what they are constantly called, what's continually declared over them, and it is also what they respond to nearly every day of their life. So not only is a name what you are called, it is who you believe you are, and so much so that you answer to it almost always. Further, what God showed me was that what people believe, what they have faith in, will manifest in their lives. Jesus said it plainly, "Be it unto you according to your faith" (Matthew 9:29). People don't just believe their name is their name, they tend to believe it is who they are. By way of example, when someone asks the question, "Who are you?" the response is generally with your name…"I am Jessica." If someone asks me, "Who are you?" I most likely would respond, "I am Siohvaughn." So names aren't just names, it represents a person's makeup, their very nature and character…whether for ill or good.

Notably, the names this king chose were all negative and quite the contrary of what God called them. Therefore, it was significant when this wicked king purported to change their names. This act was supposed to change the very nature and character of these three Hebrew boys…and for the worse. And not only that, it was intended to change what they believed about God. But God showed me plainly after reading about these boys' lives that if God is for you, nothing can truly be against you! Even though these young men were forced to answer to names that regarded them of little account, attempted to fill them with an ungodly fear, and tried to force them to worship an idol, God's declaration, and what He called them to be, could not be undone! And these young men must have had faith in God, and His love for them, that no matter how many times they were called these loathsome names, they still believed they were who God said they were, and that God is who He says He is! This is such an important lesson for us to learn, because albeit someone may never come along and legally change our name, it is very likely that someone will come along and try to change your identity and convince you that you are someone other than who God called you to be. It is vital that we know who we are in Christ. God says, we are the righteousness of God in Christ Jesus, we are the head and not the tail, above only and not beneath, God's beloved in whom He is well pleased, the bride of Christ, and as just as Jesus Christ is in the eyes of God, so are we in this world.

We have to know and believe this truth with all our heart, because there is a huge assignment from hell against believers today to get them to distort their identity in Christ in their own eyes. It takes the grace of God and faith in God to continue to believe that you are who God says you are no matter what others say about you, and regardless of whatever decisions you have made…especially ill decisions. You are not your behavior, or your mistakes; you are who God says you are. For example, you may be a person who drinks alcohol heavily right now, but you are not an alcoholic; you are the righteousness of God in Christ Jesus, and no addiction can change that. You have a choice to make—to believe what others say, or even what you say about yourself—or believe what God says, who cannot lie, when He says that you are my beloved in whom I am well pleased, because as Jesus is, so are you in this world. Our behavior can change, but God, His Word and who He says we are, will never change (Hebrew 13:8, Matthew 24:35).

The three Hebrew boys believed this truth so much that when faced with a choice between the death penalty or conforming to the God-less nature that was being forced upon them, they chose to trust in who God called them to be. And as a result, death was defied, and God was glorified! Namely, sometime after these boys had been exiled, king Nebuchadnezzar had an image of gold made and placed it in one of the provinces of Babylon. Thereafter, he commanded all the people to fall down and worship the image, and whoever refused to worship this idol would be "cast immediately into the midst of a burning fiery furnace" (Daniel 3:6). This is a very serious decree for a king to make, especially during those times, because there was no form of appeal once the decree was made. Not even the king himself was able to revoke his own decree (Daniel 6:15, Esther 8:8). Those who broke this law, had no chance of an appeal, and thus would be immediately executed upon the king's word to do so.

Well the time came for the king's decree to be executed, and thus all the peoples in that land were expected to fall down and worship the idol just as the king had commanded. However, Shadrach, Meshach, and Abed-Nego refused to bow down and worship this false god, because the King of Kings had commanded them not to (Exodus 20:4-5). The king got word of their refusal to conform and bow as their enemies had exposed their decision to the king. This had all three of these boys facing the death penalty of that day. This seems like a horrifying time but God showed me His glory in this. These boys who had continually been called of little account, fearful of God, and a worshipper of a false god, remained who God called them to be, as evinced by their refusal to bow even when faced with imminent death. They refused to cower to, or accept, becoming who others said they were, or conform their conduct to reflect the new identities this wicked king tried to force on them. Instead they remained by the very power and grace of God, who God called them, to be (Daniel 3:18). We can learn a very valuable truth here: The enemy does not possess any power at all to change our identity in Christ Jesus! You are, and always will be, who your heavenly Father says you are, and God says; "You are the righteousness of Him in Christ Jesus" (2 Corinthians 5:21).

Fireproof!

You can just about imagine how furious the prideful king was, when these three boys publically refused to worship his false god. These boys were like Jesus, in that they loved God and loved not their life even unto death. They did something that takes real strength and power from on high! They did what some of the world's strongest bodybuilding men may never be strong enough to do: They let go! At first glance, letting go doesn't seem like too much of a challenge, but if what you need to let go of, you love, or are afraid to lose, it can require the strength of God Almighty working both in and through to do it. But God, being so good, will never let you down when you let go, because you trust Him. God will never let you be put to shame (Joel 2:26).

Remember, whenever God gives you something, it takes God to bless you with that promise, and it takes God to keep that promise. This is why God will tell us to let go of the very blessings He gives, so we entrust them to His loving and all-powerful hands to keep them. This goes for health, marriage, children, ministries, careers, wealth, material possessions, and even our lives as evinced by these three Hebrew boys.

These boys understood this concept of entrusting everything to God, and therefore they let go, even when their very lives were at stake. Jesus did the same at the cross, because nobody took His life, but rather He let it go, trusting God (John 10:18). And just like Jesus, these boys didn't regret trusting God and, neither will we when we trust Him. Now, keep in mind, God will be glad you let go, and you will too, but the enemy will not, as clearly evinced by what happened next when Shadrach, Meshach, and Abed-Nego let go. Filled with rage, the king ordered not that these brave boys just be thrown into the fire, but instead he commanded that the furnace first be heated seven times hotter before finally casting them into the consuming fire (Daniel 3:19). Taking things further, the raging royalty also ordered that they be thrown into the burning fire completely dressed, in the following flammable fashions: their trousers, coats, turbans, and all the other garments they were wearing! It is evident this king really wanted to burn them up! And as is common to all rage, the pre-existing punishment wasn't enough, and therefore the king also ordered that it be trained members of his army—mighty men of valor— who bind these three boys up before throwing them into the fire. The angry king wanted to ensure they could not escape the flame. To call this king's order overkill; is an understatement! And I think we can all agree that naturally speaking, this seems to be going from bad too much worse for these three boys. Being bound meant that these boys had been rendered completely helpless. Any human effort to save themselves would have surely proved futile. When God showed me this, He also showed me that their helplessness was not a sign of their end, but rather a perfect opportunity for the glory of God to manifest. The same is true today. Often when something gets so bad that it is well beyond our human ability to do anything about it, and we are rendered helpless, God will manifest His glory and we, along with our enemies, both know and believe that God alone delivered us from our troubles!

Now, before we move on, I want to share something else the Lord showed me while meditating on the lives of these boys. The mighty men who bound them, and were responsible for throwing them into the fire, were killed instantly when they just drew near to the flame! (Daniel 3:22). This could have freaked out these sentenced sons of God. Because, if just getting close to the flame killed three mighty members of an army, it would seem absolutely certain that casting these three teenagers into the fire would surely result in their death. Notably, these boys didn't panic or change their posture of trusting the Lord. When the Lord revealed this to me, He let me know that you cannot believe that what others suffered is going to happen to you. You have to believe what God says concerning you. And God says, "No weapon formed against you shall prosper" (Isaiah 54:17). Believe that truth, because God cannot lie, and His Word doesn't return to Him void or empty, but it accomplishes whatever purpose He desires (Isaiah 55:11). Therefore, let us take our eyes off of man and let us instead fix our eyes on Jesus and all He has promised us, including: "A thousand may fall at your side and ten thousand at your right hand, but it shall not come near you!" (Psalms 91:7). Now, even though all of God's promises are true, there is still sometimes a process we go through prior to seeing God's manifested glory, as clearly evinced in the lives of these three Hebrew boys. The time finally came for the king's decree of death to be executed, and the king did in fact have them thrown into the fiery furnace to be destroyed and killed, but when they got into the fire, Jesus was "in the midst of the fire" with them, and because Jesus was in the midst, these boys were not consumed. In fact, they were completely unharmed by the fire! (Daniel 3:25). There is a most crucial truth right here for us to learn. Whenever, and wherever, Jesus is in the midst, hell and all of its fury, has no power at all to harm you! There is powerful protection when Jesus is in the midst. These boys were not only protected from the fierce flames, they didn't even smell like smoke when Jesus delivered them out of the fire (Daniel 3:27). Not only that, when Jesus was in their midst, the ties that the mighty men of valor bound these three boys with, fell off of them and they were free, even in the midst of their troubles! (Daniel 3:25). The devil has tried to convince some people that they cannot be free until they are delivered from their troubles, but the Word of God tells us clearly that is a lie. Jesus set these three boys free while the flames of trouble burned fiercely all around them. Jesus is all-powerful; whether trouble is absent or present…whether it's a little trouble or trouble that has been turned up seven times as much. God is still God, and He is still sovereign! Jesus in our midst is all we need. He is more than sufficient to meet any need and deliver us from any challenge we face.

Thus, inviting Jesus in the midst of your marriage is the wisest decision you can make married people, because no fire can consume it! Pray that Jesus be in the midst of the lives of your children, and no premature death can prevail against them. Pray for Jesus to be in the midst of your entire life, for with Him, you can flourish even in the flames of trouble, and withstand any fiery trial.

Again, it is so powerful when Jesus is in the midst. By way of example, after Jesus was crucified, His disciples were hiding because of fear of the Jews who had delivered Jesus up to be crucified (John 20:19). I'm certain these disciples thought they were next to be crucified for following Jesus, and that if they just watched the Son of God die, they would not stand a chance. Jesus, however, appeared in their midst, and soon after, all fear fled from them and faith arose in their hearts (John 20:19-20). Also, the Bible says that where two or three agree on **anything**, it will be done for them, because where two or three gather together in the name of Jesus, He is in the midst! (Matthew 18:20). Also, the Lord showed me a Bible verse that illustrates the power of God in our lives when He is in the midst. Psalm 46:5 promises that when "God is in the midst of her, she shall not be moved!" Again, there is something very powerful that happens when Jesus is in the midst!

Jesus also showed me that because He was in the three Hebrew boys midst, He not only prevented them from being burned, and freed them while in their troubles from all that bound them, but He delivered them from their trouble unharmed. In fact, the bible says that not even a single hair on their heads was singed. Further, God had the same king that sentenced them to death witness the very power of God in their lives, and order that they be taken out of the very trouble that he put them in! God will make the same people who used their mouths to curse you, turn right around and use their mouths to bless you. (And to those in prison, know that God can make the same judge that sentenced you, turn around and order your release). Our God reigns supreme!

We also see from these boys lives that God will not only protects us, He even protects our possessions. Jesus protected their clothes from the fire too! God is very good to us, loves us deeply, and has even extended His divine protection to our possessions.

"So what shall we say to these things? If God is for us, who can be against us?" (Romans 8:31). Not even an all-consuming fire! Therefore, let us hold fast to this confession of faith, without wavering, because He who promised us this is faithful to do all He promises, including protect and deliver us. And let us not fear trouble, formed weapons, or storms that arise. God is a shelter in the storm…a strong tower, where we run into and are safe. He is our mighty fortress (Proverbs 18:10). God would not need to be a mighty fortress, a shelter, or a strong tower for us, if we lived in a world where evil didn't exist; but because it does, God's divine protection surrounds us as a shield. In knowing this truth, that trouble does exist in the world we live in, but God protects us from it, we can understand and still believe that God loves us, even when He allows certain trials or troubles in our lives. God is with us and for us, so we have no reason to fear the fire of trouble. And with Jesus in our midst, we are fireproof!

God Chooses Not to Lose One

When considering why our lives take certain turns and we are allowed to go through certain challenges, we must remember that God chooses not to lose one (John 6:39). Some of you have gone through things that God allowed for the sake of others' souls. There are people who need to hear about, or otherwise witness, your miracle, because for some, their lives depend on it, and for others, their very souls. Jesus said it like this once, "Unless you people see signs and wonders you will by no means believe" (John 4:48). We see this in the life story of these three Hebrew boys as well. The king who ordered their execution had so much disdain for God that he ordered that His children be put to death for obeying Him. However, after this king witnessed Jesus in the midst of that fire, protect and deliver His children miraculously from it completely unharmed, he not only acknowledged that God was the "Most High God" but he also testified that God is the One who saved these boys out of his hands and "frustrated the king's word" (Daniel 3:26 & 28). The king went on further to issue a decree as law in that nation that "any people, nation or language which speaks anything amiss against the God of Shadrach, Meshach and Abed-Nego shall be cut in pieces, and their houses shall be made an ash heap; because there is no other God who can deliver like this" (Daniel 3:29). This king went from despising God to attempting to defend Him. The result? God is glorified! He is glorified, not only in protecting, saving, and delivering His children from the impossible odds that were against them, but also in causing the same pride-filled king who was completely against Him, to within the same day turn around and be for Him!

Now, after reading and understanding the truths God has revealed to us through their lives, we should know and believe that Jesus will deliver us and protect us in times of trouble, both for our sakes and for the sake of those who need to witness the glory of our God so that they too will believe in God. I am convinced that there are people who need the miracle we pray for, as much as we do, if not more. Therefore, if you are someone reading this who is currently facing trouble, or feel as though you have been surrounded by consuming fire please remember, God has not forgotten you. He didn't forget these three Hebrew boys, and He hasn't forgotten you. But these boys, like all of us, had to let God finish. They had to trust God and allow Him to deliver them His way and in His time. Trust God; He has a plan for you, which is good and not evil, to give you hope and a future, and no plan of God's can be thwarted (Jeremiah 29:11). Know, and believe, that if God has allowed fire in your life; this fire will not consume you. The fire isn't for your destruction; it is for the glory of God!

You are My witnesses, says the Lord, and My servant whom I have chosen, that you may know and believe Me and understand that I am He. Before Me there was no God formed, Nor shall there be after Me. I, even I, am the Lord, and besides Me there is no savior." (Isaiah 43:10-11)

CHAPTER 6:

GOD WILL DELIVER YOU

Your God…He will deliver you. (Daniel 6:16)

GOD'S HEART FOR US IS SO BEAUTIFUL. HE IS FOREVER MIND-
ful of us and whatever challenges we face, and it is His deep desire
that we know how much He loves us and have understanding of
His ways, so that we will not despair when trouble comes. The Lord
showed me that there are many believers who are either on the brink
of despair, or full-fledged in it because they lack understanding of
how God is moving in their lives. And because of His untiring love
for us, God has sent me to reveal His love for us and His plan to
deliver us so that we don't give up. Specifically, the Lord showed me
that there are believers who need to be delivered and no matter what
they have tried, or who they know, they are not delivered. This has
caused them to be frustrated, confused, and question God's love and
whether or not He will set them free. God has sent me to tell you
not to despair, because He does love you and He will deliver you!
You don't have to be frustrated any longer because of people who

won't help you. There is a reason for this. The reason people have not wanted to help you, or those who wanted to help you are not able to, is because God Himself wants to deliver you. God wants you, and everyone around you, to know that He delivered you out of all your distresses. This is because for God, it is more important that you have revelation of who He is than it is for you to just be delivered from your troubles. Therefore, God wants to and will deliver you Himself! And in doing so you will know God is your Deliverer! So, instead of feeling despair or frustration, rejoice. God Himself has come to deliver you!

This is what God did for Daniel. And the Lord wants to expound on His Word, and His ways via the life of Daniel in order to reveal Himself as the God who comes personally in order to deliver His people out of the hands of their enemies, so we know that God will indeed deliver us. But like Daniel, we gotta let God finish!

Persecution with a Purpose

I am so glad that God opens up the book of Daniel revealing to us that Daniel is a faithful servant of God...but as faithful as Daniel was, he still faced serious trouble and challenges. This is good news, because too often the enemy, and people who are erroneously filled with religion, will try to convince a Christian that the trouble they are faced with is because of something they did wrong. We see this in the Gospel of John when Jesus healed a blind man. The Bible says it like this: "Now as Jesus passed by He saw a man who was blind from birth. And His disciples asked Him, saying, 'Rabbi, *who sinned*, this man or his parents, that he was born blind?' Jesus answered, 'Neither this man nor his parents sinned, but that the works should be revealed in him'" (John 9:1-3). Notably, Jesus wasn't faultfinding, but the question from the disciples back then is indicative of the mindset of many others today. If someone faces a crisis, they conclude that there must be sin in their life…or even in their parents' life that caused it. But for the believer, because of Jesus Christ' death, remitting all of our sins, and His resurrection, making us righteous before God; the issue of sin is now obsolete! Hallelujah!

Thus, when it comes to generational curses, God says: "Christ has redeemed us from the curse of the law." Jesus has made sure that sin and the curse therefrom are no longer issues between us and God! In the gracious and powerful words of our Savior, "It is finished!" (John 19:30). Therefore, let us cease from the sin search when trouble arises and resist the devil and his lying accusations that the sin you committed is the reason for the adversity you are facing. Instead, let us search the scriptures for the truth: All our sins have been forgiven and we are righteous in the sight of God! God Himself has made us righteous, and we know that whatever God does, cannot be undone!

Now, that said, we must know that righteousness doesn't exempt us from trouble. What it does do, however, is guarantee our deliverance from any trouble! It is written, "Many are the afflictions of the righteous but the Lord delivers him from them all" (Psalm 34:19). So God's promise isn't avoidance of trouble, but deliverance when it comes. Daniel was no exception to this rule. He walked upright before God, but due to envy of his excellency, he was persecuted heavily. The Bible says that Daniel distinguished himself from all the other kings' servants because he had a spirit of excellency in him, and even his enemies acknowledged that no fault or error could be found in him (Daniel 1:3-4). God had filled Daniel with a spirit of excellency and faithfulness so much so, that King Darius, whom Daniel served in those days, sought to promote Daniel over the entire realm of his kingdom (Daniel 6:3).

This promotion didn't come without persecution, however. Some of the other leaders gathered together to find a way to destroy him, so that he would never see that promotion. That was their evil purpose behind the persecution. But thanks be to God, who sits high and looks low, keeping a close eye on His beloved at all times, working everything together for our good, and having a divine purpose… even for persecution that comes our way. Now, because Daniel had a spirit of excellency, his enemies concluded that the only way to carry out their evil plan was to use Daniel's relationship and faithfulness to God as their means (Daniel 6:5). This is proof that hell was involved in this wicked plan. The enemy came directly against Daniel's relationship with God. Namely, he used those envious men to deceive the king and get him to issue a decree, which forbade any prayer and worship to any god, and instead decreed that people should worship King Darius. The penalty for not doing so was to be put to death by being thrown into the lions' den (Daniel 6:7). These men knew that Daniel was faithful to God and prayed faithfully three times a day, and they knew he would not cease even if it meant death.

After the king issued the decree, as Daniel's enemies suspected, Daniel continued to be faithful to God and prayed. And when he did, his adversaries were waiting in the wings to accuse him and drag him before the king so that the king would have no choice but to enforce his irrevocable decree (Daniel 6:15). And so it was that King Darius, even though he didn't have a heart to destroy Daniel, had an unbending law before him, which commanded Daniel be put to death for breaking it. Nevertheless, the king's love for Daniel caused him to labor to find another way for Daniel to be delivered from the lions' den. But with all his authority, wise counselors, and even his love for Daniel, he could not deliver him. No, there was not one who was able to find a way for Daniel to be delivered from the lions' den, not even Daniel…and Daniel had the wisdom of God in him.

When the Lord showed me this, He showed me how similar circumstances arise in our lives. There are times when God won't allow anyone to deliver us but Him alone. He reserves our deliverance for Himself and won't use a human vessel to help. This can be scary, and without understanding, despairing. It is one thing for someone to not want to help you get out of trouble, but it can get scary when there are people who want to help, but can't. But thanks be to God who never forsakes us, and wants to come personally to deliver us. This is good news! This is a privilege and Daniel was blessed to have it.

Once the king realized his heartfelt, yet human, efforts were futile and he couldn't save Daniel, he humbled himself and said to Daniel, "Your God whom you serve continually, He will deliver you" (Daniel 6:16). There is so much power in humility! King Darius let go and he let God. And we will soon see the power in doing that.

Sorrowfully, the king had Daniel cast into the lions' den and a stone was brought and placed on the mouth of the den, and the king sealed it with his signet ring. Daniel was as good as dead in that den with hungry lions. The next day, however, when the king went in haste to the lions' den saying, "Daniel, servant of the living God, has your God, whom you serve continually, been able to deliver you from the lions?" He found that indeed God Himself had delivered Daniel. God caused the mouths of the lions to be shut so they did Daniel no harm at all! (Daniel 6:22). God reserved this supernatural deliverance for Himself, excluding all human efforts, and thus retaining all the glory for who it truly belongs to... God alone!

Now we see that there was divine purpose for the persecution. Mankind was humbled and God was highly exalted. Not only that, but God drew Daniel's enemies out and exposed them, too. Something covered up doesn't get dealt with, but when it is exposed, it can be exterminated like it needs to be. Oh, the infinite wisdom of our God! Once, these evil men's hearts were exposed, King Darius issued a new decree and put them in the same lions' den they plotted to put Daniel in, but their sentence was worse. These evil men, their wives, and their children were all put to death in the lions' den. We have to understand that this extermination of these wicked men meant long life for Daniel, and that the purpose of God for Daniel's life would be fulfilled. God wasn't just fighting for Daniel, He was fighting for his purpose and all the lives Daniel would continue to impact for God's glory and their good…including you and me. God's heart for us is one of love, and God in His infinite wisdom goes before us working all things together for our good. Thus, we can trust God's purpose… even His purpose for allowing persecution. It is not for our destruction, but for God's glory, the increase of our faith, and to draw the enemy out so that he is destroyed forever in our lives!

God Is Our Defender

I feel pressed upon to share with you another liberating truth God taught me through the life of Daniel: God is our Defender! And because God is almighty, He won't be needing our help. That's humbling, but it's also the truth. A liberating truth that brings rest. A truth, we as children of God, need to let sink down deep inside of us, and take root. Especially, since it seems to be human nature to want to defend ourselves. But we must understand that there is no power at all in us taking up our own case, and defending ourselves…the power is in submitting unto God, resisting the devil, and allowing God alone to defend us. In this context, submitting unto God is trusting Him to defend us and resting in Him while He does. Resisting the devil in this context means resisting the temptation to fear that God won't help us, which causes us to get into all sorts of human failing attempts to deliver ourselves. We cannot deliver ourselves, because we are not the Deliverer. And because God sustains this whole world and everything above it and beneath without our help, it is safe to say, He can resolve any problems we have, without our help. After all, He is **Almighty** God, and we are mankind whose breath is in his nostrils. (I told you this was a humbling truth…but a necessary one.)

I learned this truth the hard way. I've been friends with someone for years, and the enemy, along with our flesh, caused a small flame of disagreement to turn into a raging fire of fights. God told me very clearly to close my mouth and don't defend myself. He said to me time and time again, "I will defend you." I didn't see this defense fast enough and let pride creep in, telling me I didn't deserve to be treated the way I was being treated, and I would set this friend straight for disrespecting me. The result? The relationship was consumed. What was left after the fire? Ashes. I learned pretty quickly that fires don't put out fires. God told us what does. It is written, "A soft answer turns away wrath" (Proverbs 15:1). Sadly, I gained this wisdom while standing in a pile of ashes. But thanks be to God, who takes ashes and turns them into beauty. However, just because God takes messes and turns them into miracles does not mean you should want to endure the pains of unnecessary processes. I learned the hard way, but you can just learn from me… let God defend you, and cease from trying to defend yourself.

God's power and ability to defend us, without our help, is seen well in the life of Daniel. Daniel, did not try to save himself, nor could he; however, Daniel was delivered and defended in such a way that he wouldn't need to be defended from those adversaries ever again! Not only that, the promotion God had for him was still for him, and he continued to prosper (Daniel 6:26). After, God revealed to King Darius how he had been deceived in issuing a decree which could have killed Daniel, he ordered the execution all Daniel's enemies and their families (in case they wanted to later come an avenge the wicked). By the time God displayed His glory in Daniel's life both Daniel and the king knew very well that God is a Defender. And as a result a total transformation took place in King Darius. The same king who had just appealed to his own pride, causing him to enter a decree forcing people to worship him or die, turned around and said, "I make a decree…that men must tremble and fear before the **God** of Daniel. For **He** is the living **God**, and steadfast forever; **His** kingdom is the one, which shall not be destroyed, and **His** dominion shall endure to the end. **He** delivers and rescues, and **He** works signs and wonders in heaven and on earth, **who** has delivered Daniel from the power of the lion" (Daniel 6:26-27). One move from God, and King Darius went from self-worship and self-occupation to total worship of, and complete focus on, our God! Could it be that God's decision to deliver you Himself, will cause the unbelieving onlookers to repent and believe in the only true and living God, and be completely transformed like King Darius was?

Daniel is far from being the only example of God as our Defender. Throughout the entire Bible, God reveals Himself as a mighty Defender. One example is seen in the life of King David, who God promised the throne to and assured him that from his line would come One who sits on the throne forever (Jesus) (2 Samuel 7:13). King David, like Daniel, found favor with God and man, and the persecution began. His predecessor, King Saul, was filled with envy and murderous rage toward David. Saul sought to kill David time and time again, and literally chased him away from his destiny, as David fled out of Jerusalem, where the throne was, and into the wilderness running for his life (1 Samuel 23:14). David understood, however, that God was his mighty Defender. God had saved David when he was a shepherd from ravenous beasts (1 Samuel 17:34-36). King David didn't try to defend or deliver himself, although God had given him the neck of his enemy (1 Samuel 24:4). Many times David would have been able to sneak up on a sleeping Saul and slit his throat, but David refused. The result? God took care of King Saul in such a way that David had rest all around took the throne and reigned righteously before God (2 Samuel 2:4). David let God defend him because he understood this powerful truth: "When my enemies turn back, they shall fall and perish at Your presence. For You have maintained my right and my cause" (Psalm 9:3-4). You see, as a child of God, David was God's responsibility, not David's. God promised David he would be king and it was God's responsibility to make sure that promise came to pass on the earth as it already was in heaven.

The same is true for us who God has made a promise to. And God has made many promises to every Christian. If you haven't gotten a prophetic Word, no worries. The Bible is filled with sure promises from God to every believer. It is written, all the promises of God are yes and amen in Christ. This is good news, because when God releases His Word, He is faithful to watch over it and perform it! (Jeremiah 1:12). God is the One who makes sure His promises come to pass in our lives. God did this for David, and sure enough David sat on the throne ruling...and from his line Jesus came and is seated as King of Kings forever! Clearly, God is able, willing, and delights to defend us...and He doesn't need our help; therefore beloved, rest and rejoice.

The Savior's Hidden Heart Revealed

Indeed, inside the life of Daniel is the hidden heart of our Savior Jesus Christ. Specifically, Daniel is a type of Jesus Christ. There was a law, like the law of God, in that it could not be broken without penalty of death. The Bible says, the wages of sin, or transgression against the law, is death. However, because the gift of God is eternal life, God sent His Son to die in our place. Just like King Darius was just in executing the law, but also had a heart of love toward Daniel, likewise God is just and He had to execute His judgments, but because of His love for us, He provided the way of escape for all of us who believe in His Son Jesus. Jesus is the Way, and because of His death on the cross, we Christians are surely saved. And furthermore, because of His resurrection, we are justified! Daniel's going into the lions' den, is a type of death that represents Jesus death on the cross. Daniel went into the lion's den in order to fulfill the unbending law of the king, like Jesus went to the cross to fulfill the law of God, which cannot be broken. And Daniel's being brought out of the lions' den by the king represents God resurrecting Jesus from the dead! The king's labor to find a way to deliver the one he loved is an exemplary display of God's untiring love that found a way for us to be saved, except God was well able to provide. Our Father, and His Son's heart, is one of unconditional love for us. God has already proven that He will do whatever it takes for the one He loves. Beloved, you are the one He loves!

In Closing

Again, I say, I am so glad that God used the life of Daniel to reveal Himself as the one who delivers us out of every trouble, because Daniel was a well-behaved man, but he still faced trouble. Now we can know and believe that trouble arising in our life as believers can be wholly apart from our behavior. This is important, because during trying times it is even more vital that we set our focus on Jesus, our Deliverer, and not ourselves and whether we dotted every "i" and crossed every "t." We must believe and meditate on this truth: God will deliver us regardless. However, like Daniel, we have to let God finish. Don't be discouraged because of persecution, or things seeming to go from bad to worse. Know that if God allowed it, He has a divine purpose for it, and it is for your good. If it appears that the wicked have carried out their wicked scheme and got what they wanted don't worry just let God finish. I don't say this by my own might or power, but by God's Holy Spirit: God will certainly have the last word in your life and it is good! Set your face like flint and meditate on this truth that King David understood and believed: "Do not fret because of evildoers…Rest in the Lord, and wait patiently for Him; do not fret because of him who prospers in his way, because of the man who brings wicked schemes to pass… the salvation of the righteous is from the Lord; He is their strength in the time of trouble and the Lord shall help them and deliver them; He shall deliver them from the wicked and save them" (Psalm 37:1,

7, & 39-40). Beloved, you can rest and rejoice knowing for certain that God will deliver you...your part is to let God finish!

> The righteous cry out... the Lord hears, and delivers them out of all their troubles. (Psalm 34:17)

CHAPTER 7:

JESUS LOVES YOU

God demonstrates His own love toward us, in that while
we were still sinners, Christ died for us. (Romans 5:8)

OF ALL THE TESTIMONIES GOD DECIDED TO USE IN THIS BOOK,
the lives of Martha, Mary, and Lazarus I can most closely relate to.
These three believed in Jesus, loved Him, knew and believed He
loved them, yet had their faith tested in a most major way (John 11).
What they prayed and hoped for died. Every bit of hope seemed to
be lost, and Jesus seemed to be late. I can relate! It was at a time like
this, when God taught me that it isn't our love for Jesus that sees us
through these most difficult times, it is a revelation of, and faith in,
Jesus' love for us that does. In dead circumstances, and hopeless sit-
uations, we must do what the Holy Spirit led Mary and Martha to do,
and that is meditate on, believe, and confess that the Lord loves us.

Perhaps you are someone who is currently facing what appears
to be a dead situation, or have done so in your past. May the Lord's
heart of love, as it is revealed through the lives of Martha, Mary, and

Lazarus, cause you to know and believe His unfailing love for you, and may His perfect love heal, restore, and set you free from any pain, loss, fear, and confusion caused by very trying times.

The Power of Believing and Confessing Jesus Loves Me

Again, Martha, Mary, and Lazarus were believers, who loved Jesus. More importantly, they believed that the Lord loved them. Therefore, when their brother Lazarus became very ill, and was facing death due to the illness, they cried out to Jesus to come and heal him. The challenge they faced was a matter of life and death, and what these women did during this most trying time, we can learn from and mirror whenever we are faced with adversity…and we likewise can receive the miracle we pray for.

First, these women prayed and cried out to Jesus for help. We too, should cry out to Jesus because the eyes of the Lord are upon the righteous and His ears are open to their cry (Psalms 34:15). And remember, believers, you are the righteousness of God in Christ Jesus. Also, God promises, "the effective, fervent prayer of a righteous man avails much" (James 5:16). Jesus said it this way, "You did not chose Me, but I chose you and appointed you that you should go and bear fruit and that your fruit should remain, that *whatever you ask the Father in My name, He may give you*" (John 15:16). Also, Jesus promises, "Ask, and it will be given you; seek, and you will find; knock, and it will be opened to you. For everyone who asks receives, and he who seeks finds, and to him who knocks it will be opened" (Matthew 7:7-8). The Bible is filled with promises from the Lord that He does in fact answer our prayers. Therefore, let us, like these two women Martha and Mary, "come boldly to the throne of grace where we may obtain mercy and find grace to help in time of need" (Hebrews 4:15).

The Lord also showed me that these women did something else powerful and wise, when faced with adversity. At the early onset of their trying time, Martha and Mary meditated on, believed, and confessed the Lord's love for them (John 11:3). We should learn and apply this same wisdom. At the moment trouble comes to us, meditate on, believe, and confess this truth: Jesus loves me. If it is a loved one of yours who is in trouble, the same wisdom applies: Meditate on, believe, and confess aloud that Jesus loves them. This is very important, because Jesus told us time and time again when it comes to facing trouble; our part is to "Only believe" (Luke 8:50). In order to believe, you must have faith, and because God is so good He has given to each one of us a measure of faith (Romans 12:3). And if someone needs more faith, faith comes by hearing, and hearing the Word of Christ (Romans 10:17). And the Word of Christ Himself is: He loves us, and God loves us just like He loves Jesus (John 16:27). Therefore, when we are confessing Jesus loves us, we are confessing the Word of Christ, and when we confess it out loud, we hear the Word of Christ, and when we hear the Word of Christ, God's promised faith comes…and when faith comes, we believe. And when we believe; we receive. And when we receive; mountains move and even the dead are raised! Mountains representing those circumstances whereby the trouble seems bigger than us, and too much for us to handle. Death representing those hopeless circumstances, where it seems like it is over, defeat has set in, and it's too late to do anything about it. But again, God is so good, that whether it's a mountain we face, death, or anything else, His instruction for us remains the same: "Only believe." Therefore, we can see why it is both wise and powerful to not only meditate on and believe that Jesus loves us, but to also speak the Word of Christ aloud, thereby hearing it, and thus causing faith to come.

Another benefit of faith coming is that faith protects us from the fiery darts of the enemy. God said, "taking up the shield of **faith** with which you will be able to quench all the fiery darts of the wicked one (Ephesians 6:16). These fiery darts during a trial usually include doubt and unbelief, which the devil uses in his desperate, and fear-filled, attempt to get us to give up on God, and not believe that God will do what He promised. But we know that nothing could be further from the truth, because Jesus always does what He promises and He cannot lie! (Jeremiah 1:12). Faith in this truth protects us from doubt and unbelief and we receive the miracle we are asking for.

Also, the Holy Spirit showed me that God specifically said to **take up** the shield of faith, because when it is taken up, it covers the head and the heart. One of the reasons God uses the shield of faith to cover our head is because this whole battle of faith versus unbelief takes place in the mind. This is because Jesus defeated the devil and he has no power at all to defeat us, and so the enemy attacks our mind with lies, doubt, and fear to get us to defeat ourselves, by believing his lies instead of God's unfailing truths. When the shield of faith is taken up, therefore, it protects our mind from these desperate attacks from this defeated foe.

Also, the shield of faith covers our heart, because when the enemy lies to us, telling us that God is a lie, and won't do what He promised, we can feel bitter and hard in our hearts toward God, which produces an inability to truly receive or give love. The Bible says very clearly "we love, because [God] first loved us" (1 John 4:19). Therefore, when we don't believe God loves us, it robs us of the ability to love others and Jesus emphasized the importance of us loving one another. Jesus knows how important it is for us to love one another as New Covenant believers. In fact Jesus said the entire law is summed up in this: "Love one another" (Galatians 5:14). Not only is loving one another important for that reason, but also because when you give love, you give God, for God is love…and wherever God is, there is freedom, protection and great power. This helps put in perspective how vital it is to take up the shield of faith.

Also, the importance of taking up the shield of faith is shown by what Jesus said just before being crucified. The Lord said, "Peace

I leave with you, My peace I give to you…Let not your heart be troubled, neither let it be afraid" (John 14:27). It seems as though we can truly experience Jesus' very own peace (which by the way allowed Him to sleep soundly inside of a boat that was nearly capsized) if we don't allow our hearts to be troubled or afraid (John 14:1). I don't know about you, but I absolutely want to possess this peace that allows you to sleep when the situation screams, "You're sinking!" Faith plays a major role in having this peace manifest in our lives and peace resides in our hearts and minds. Thus, when we take up the shield of faith it covers and protects the peace of God that is shed abroad in our minds and hearts. And these are just some of the benefits of having faith, and they are in and of themselves life altering!

Now, not only is it important for us to meditate on, believe, and confess the love Jesus has for the preceding reasons, it is also vital because we don't always understand what's happening, or why God allows certain circumstances to transpire the way they do, when facing a trial. This too is illustrated in the lives of Martha, Mary, and Lazarus when they faced their trial. After they sent for Jesus, saying, "Lord behold, he whom You love [Lazarus] is sick," Jesus heard their prayer, and He said to them, "This sickness is not unto death, but for the glory of God, that the Son of Man be glorified through it" (John 11:4, emphasis mine). After Jesus gave them this Word, the Bible states, "Now, Jesus loved Martha and her sister and Lazarus. So when He heard that he was sick, **He stayed two more days** in the place where He was" (John 11:5). Keep in mind that everything written in the Bible is for our benefit (Romans 15:4). The Holy Spirit made sure that it was written down for us that "… Jesus loved Martha and her sister and Lazarus." Because God also records that Jesus, albeit He heard Martha and Mary's prayers to come and heal their dying brother, He stayed two more days where He was. God wants us to know that even if it seems like Jesus heard your prayer, but isn't answering or it is too late; Jesus does love you. And keep in mind that Jesus can never be late, because Jesus created time, and the created is never greater than the Creator. Time serves God; God doesn't serve time! Therefore, humanly speaking you may be out of time, but if you are praying to Jesus, He can create more time, or make time obsolete and completely unnecessary to answer your prayers. Let that truth sink real deep down on the inside of you, because it is a most vital truth during a trying time. Now, granted if you were Jesus, you may have handled things differently for Martha, her sister, and Lazarus, but just because of that fact doesn't make the way the Lord chose to go about resolving the matter wrong, and it certainly doesn't mean He is unloving. In fact, the exact opposite is true. It was because of Jesus' love that He did what He did, the way He did it for them. And regarding His ways of handling matters; the Bible says, "Oh, the depth of the riches both of the wisdom and knowledge of God! How unsearchable are His judgments and His ways past finding out!" (Romans 11:33), and the ways of God are higher than ours (Isaiah 55:9). Therefore, we may never understand fully the ways of God on this side of heaven, but we can know and believe that they are enriched with both wisdom and love beyond any human understanding We need to be mindful of this truth when going through a difficult time, because God doesn't always resolve matters the way we think He should. But He always resolves them much better! Knowing this truth, we can further know and believe that Jesus does love us, no matter what challenge we are faced with, or how God choses to resolve it.

Now, the members of this family weren't the only people of God who had this powerful revelation about meditating on and confessing the love of God for you when trouble arises. King Jehoshaphat, King of Israel, was suddenly given news one day that the people of Moab, Ammon and others with them, were all coming against Jehoshaphat (2 Chronicles 20:1-2). This wise king, although afraid of the threat against his life and the lives of his people, cried out to the Lord, asked his people to pray, and fasted. God sent a prophet to Jehoshaphat to tell him these powerful words, which God is still saying to His children today: "Do not be afraid nor dismayed because of this great multitude, for the battle is not yours, but God's…You will not need to fight in this battle. Position yourselves, stand still and see the salvation of the Lord, who is with you" (2 Chronicles 20:15 & 17). The truth is, the battle is the Lord's and the Lord has won the battle already, He just bestows upon us the victory and the benefits therefrom. Therefore, we can rest, beloved. It is finished! When Jehoshaphat heard these words from God through His prophet, he worshipped God and charged the people with the wisdom of God to go to the battlefield singing songs confessing the goodness and love of God for them. They sang out, "Praise the Lord, for His mercy [loving kindness in Hebrew] endures forever" (2 Chronicles 20:21). The result of these people believing and confessing God's love for them during times of trial and tribulation was that when they arrived at the battlefield, they realized that all of the armies that came against them had killed one another, and Jehoshaphat and the children of God spent the next three days collecting all the gold and riches off the dead bodies of their enemies! They didn't have to fight; they just had to have a revelation of God's love for them and confess it! God is the same, beloved, and what He did for Jehoshaphat He desires to do for every one of His children. Therefore, let us meditate on, believe, and confess this powerful truth: God loves us!

When the Word is All You Have
The Word is All You Need

God also told me that Jesus did provide Martha, Mary, and Lazarus with what they needed when they prayed. And what they needed was not for Jesus to come and heal Lazarus at the moment they cried out…they needed the Word. Jesus gave them His Word to hear and believe while they let God finish! Jesus said to them, "This sickness is not unto death, but for the glory of God, so the Son of

God will be glorified through it" (John 11:4). It was Jesus love for them that caused Him to provide to this family with exactly what they needed at that moment of their trying times. But they needed faith to believe that was true.

Likewise, we at times may pray and cry out to God, and it seems like Jesus refrained from doing the miracle we need, but He gives His Word of promise so that we will know and believe that He hears us, and He will answer us above and beyond what we have prayed for. Now, remember Jesus' Word to us isn't just an encouraging word, although it results in us being encouraged. It is the absolute sovereign and unfailing Word of God Himself! It is certain to come to pass. Jesus doesn't mutter wishful thinking, Jesus declares to us the end of a thing, because He determined the end in the beginning and knows exactly how these trials will turn out (Isaiah 46:10). To add to that, God cannot lie. It's not that God doesn't want to lie, for even that would be somewhat of a relief, but for God, lying is simply impossible; and in that we can have perfect peace! Thus, if you have a Word from God (and the Bible is full of them for Christians), it doesn't matter if your situation has died, the power of God's Word will resurrect it!

Additionally, whenever God sends His Word out, it cannot come back to Him void or empty, but it must prosper in the thing for which He sent it. And indeed, in the lives of Martha, Mary, and Lazarus, this is exactly what happened, and it will happen in your life too as long as you do what they did…let God finish! It's not over unless God says it's over, and God will have the final say in your life and in all circumstances concerning your life! After all, Jesus is the Alpha and the Omega, He is, the beginning and the end! (Revelation 22:13). So, if a word from God is all you have; know the word from God is all you need!

It Takes Faith to Receive Your Miracle

One day while visiting with my mom, I began to reflect on a prayer I made, and how it *seemed* as though God had answered my prayer...and He had answered it even faster than I expected. And while this seems to be good news, and a sure reason to celebrate, I realized I didn't really believe God had answered my prayer. So instead of celebrating, I was doubtful and confused. It was at that moment that God showed me this truth; it takes faith to believe that you have received your miracle from God. The Lord began revealing this truth to me by allowing me to see my own hesitation to believe that God answered my prayer. I knew God heard my prayers and I allowed God to finish, but when He handed me the answer; I doubted that He did. The Lord then confirmed to me through the lives of Martha and Mary this same truth...it takes faith to receive your miracle. They too struggled with this same issue as I did. Now, keep in mind that the Lord isn't revealing this to us to condemn us, but rather He is revealing the truth so that the truth will set us free and the Lord wants us ready to receive our answer.

Now, Martha and Mary had prayed for Jesus to come and heal their brother while he was still alive and fighting a deadly sickness, and it seemed as though Jesus had not answered their prayers, because Lazarus died (John 11:17). Four days after Lazarus was in his grave, Jesus came to the town where Martha and Mary were... and where Lazarus had been buried. Let's be real, Jesus showing up four days after a funeral seems as though He is too late. This is why I admire the measure of faith the Lord gave Martha. Indeed, she had a measure of great faith in Jesus. Even after Lazarus was dead for four days, **as soon as Martha heard** Jesus was coming, she came to Him and said, "Lord if you had been here my brother would not have died, **but even now** I know that **whatever You ask of God, God will give you**" (John 11:22). Martha, after knowing, believing, and confessing the love Jesus has for her and her family, had enough faith in the Lord's love and goodness to dare to believe four days after a funeral, is still not too late for Jesus to raise the deadest situation! She was essentially saying to Jesus, Lord, you can fix even the deadest circumstance, because You love us, and You have the power to do so! We have to believe the same, no matter how dead the circumstance seems to be, or how long it has been in a tomb.

Now, after Martha had expressed those words of faith to Jesus, He responded to Martha's faith by telling her, "Your brother will rise again" (John 11:23). Martha then answered, "I know that he will rise again in the resurrection and the **last day**" (John 11:24). She went from saying "even now" to the "last day." This lets us know that even though we can have great faith in God, as humans we may waiver in that faith. Martha is human like the rest of us and she did just that. Now, Jesus in His love and tenderness toward Martha (and toward us, because He is using her life to teach us many things about Himself), responded by saying, "**I am** the resurrection and the life. He who believes in Me, though he may die, he shall live. And whoever lives and believes in Me shall never die. Do you believe this?" (John 11:25). Jesus was letting her (as well as us) know that it's not about how dead a circumstance is, or about how long it's been that way. It's not about what should have happened (Lord, if only you had been here) and it's not about what could happen in the future (the last day), but I am right now, no matter what, everything you need! God says, "I am, that I am!" (Exodus 3:14). This is good news, beloved! Have no regard for the severity of the circumstance, what could have happened, or for tomorrow…just know and believe that Jesus is your "I am." He is your **ever-present** help in time of trouble! Have no regard for the time. Jesus created all things, including time and remember that Jesus doesn't serve time, time serves Jesus. If it is more time you need, more time you will get from the Lord! It can never be too late for the owner of time and your God, Jesus Christ, owns all things, including time! Therefore, let God be who He is to you. He is all you need and want right now!

After Jesus had said all these things to Martha, she responded, "Yes, Lord I believe" (John 11:27). Mary then heard that Jesus had come and was calling for her, and "as soon as she heard that," she rose up and went quickly toward Jesus. Jesus, seeing Mary weep, and the others with her weep, began to weep with them (John 11:35). The Lord then went where they had laid Lazarus, and commanded that the stone in front of Lazarus' tomb be taken away (John 11: 38). Now, remember the Lord promised them "This sickness is not unto death but for the glory of God, that the Son of God may be glorified in it" and He is there at Lazarus' tomb having the stone that holds Lazarus hostage rolled away. In other words, the Word is there to fulfill His Word to them,, but the response was "Lord, by this time there is a stench, for he has been dead four days" (John 11:39). Notice in the response she mentions Lazarus' death and how long he's been dead. This God showed me is a problem that still invokes doubt in some today. The enemy wants our mind on how dead the circumstance seems to be and just how long it has been that way, so that even when God is answering the prayers we made, we won't see it, having been blinded by doubt. But God in His love for us is setting us free with the truth even right now, as He did for them back then. The Lord said, "Did I not say to you that if you would believe you would see the glory of God?" (John 11:40). We have come back full circle with God. Jesus is making it abundantly clear, no matter how dead a situation gets, or how long it's been in the grave, only believe and you will see the glory of God! Thus, Martha and Mary didn't just need faith to believe Jesus would answer their prayer; they needed faith to receive their miracle when God was answering them. The same is true for us today as children of God.

Next, Jesus prayed to God aloud for our sakes, and theirs, and afterwards with just three words, the Lord said, "Lazarus, come forth," and a man who had been dead for four whole days arose like he had only taken a cat nap! People of God, let's settle this once and for all. It is of no importance how bad something is, or how long it's been in that condition; Jesus with three words is undoing death sentences that have been fully carried out! Our God reigns!!! Let us therefore believe Jesus will definitely answer us, and have no more regard for the circumstance or its severity, because none of that is a match for our God!

No More Complacency

Before completely leaving this subject matter—about having faith to receive your miracle—I want to share with you something the Lord showed me was opposing the believer from having faith to receive his or her miracle...complacency. The Lord showed me that this creeps in when someone has been waiting a long time for the answer to his or her prayers.

To illustrate this truth, Jesus showed me the life of a man in the Bible who was paralyzed for thirty-eight years, demonstrating just how complacency can try to hinder someone from receiving the answer to their prayers. During this man's lifetime in Jerusalem there was beside a certain Sheep Gate, a pool. And beside this pool there lay "a great multitude of sick people, blind, lame, paralyzed, waiting for the moving of the water" because at a certain time an angel would come and stir up the water, and whoever went into the stirred water first was healed of whatever affliction they had (John 5). One day, the man who had been paralyzed for thirty-eight years was lying beside the pool, waiting for the angel to come and stir the water, in order for him to be healed...like he did day after day for a long time. Without question this lame man had faith to believe that God exists, and that God heals. This is evinced by the fact that he continually lay beside that pool day after day for a multitude of years, in order to get healed by an angel God sent into the waters. So we see, he had faith that God exists and faith that God heals, however, when it came to having faith to actually receive his miracle, he lacked it. Jesus, who is without doubt, the answer to all prayer, came to where the man was, saw him lying there, and acknowledged that he had been with that condition for a long time (John 5:6). Interestingly, Jesus then asked the man did he want to be healed. The man responded, "Sir I have no man to put me into the pool when the water is stirred up; so while I am coming, another steps down before me" (John 5:7). Amazingly, the man didn't even answer the question; he just spoke about all the things that opposed him receiving the answer to his prayer. He had more faith in the problem than in the Solution. Christ Jesus is the Solution and He was right there asking him if he wanted to be healed. And instead of him responding yes Lord, I receive my miracle; he just kept on discussing the problem. It was then when Jesus told me to take notice that this man hadn't just waited on his prayer to be answered, but he had waited "a long time" and that long time waiting played a major role in him struggling to receive the miracle he prayed for. He had become complacent with the problem. The Lord let me know He was revealing this to us so that we don't get complacent with the problem while waiting for the Solution. Waiting may be a part of some journeys with God, but it is never the destination with Him.

Death Is An Enemy of God's

Another truth God showed me via the lives of Martha, Mary, and Lazarus was this: death is an enemy of God's. The Bible says, "The last *enemy* to be destroyed is death" (1 Corinthians 15:26). So, if you have lost someone you love, know that Jesus wept with you as you mourned, just like He did with these sisters, because Jesus loves you too. But you may be thinking, Jesus didn't raise my family member from the dead, like He did Lazarus, and so how can He love me like He loved them? You are right, Jesus didn't do the same for you, He did better for you. For the Bible tells us that the believer passes from death to life and dies again no more (1 John 3:14). Your family member didn't suffer the sting of death, but passed from death into everlasting life! This is good news. Also, some of Lazarus' loved ones had to endure his funeral twice, and I don't know about you, but one funeral for a loved one is enough! Not only that, but when Lazarus was raised from the dead, he was back in the same world where sickness and death exist. Your family member, who fell asleep, woke up, and saw Jesus Christ face to face, received a new body, was escorted into the unhindered presence of God in heaven, surrounded by loved ones who went home before them, and off to the mansion that Jesus prepared for them...to forever live in perfect peace and everlasting joy. Jesus definitely provided you with a greater miracle for you loved ones and He did so because He loves you, loves them and counts death an enemy.

You Will Not Be Put to Shame!

Notice how God allowed people around Martha and Mary to witness their trying time, and see them when it looked like the God they served was too late. This was not for their shame, but for the glory of God, so that these spectators would also believe that Jesus is the resurrection and the life. In doing so, when the those onlookers are faced with a trial, or a dead circumstance, they will know to call on the God of Mary, Martha, and Lazarus to have even the deadest of things resurrected! Perhaps you, like myself, have wondered why God allowed people to witness your most difficult times, especially since that can be a trial in and of itself. Well, it certainly isn't to shame you. God has promised, "Do not fear, for you will not be ashamed. Neither be disgraced..." (Isaiah 54:4). And again, God promised, "My people shall never be put to shame" (Joel 2:26). Therefore, know and believe that God hasn't allowed the onlookers to see you in defeat...

He has had their eyes turned toward you, because that is exactly where He is manifesting His glory!

In Closing

I thank God for using Martha, Mary and Lazarus' lives as an example for us, in times of trial. We see that they prayed, believed the Lord loved them, confessed the Lord's love for them, and even waited, but their prayers seemed to go unanswered. What more could anyone do? The answer is now what it was then: You gotta let God finish! And we know that the fuel it takes to let God finish is faith. We also know that faith comes by hearing, and hearing the Word of Christ. And because God loves you and is for you, He has led you to hear the word of Christ through this book and faith has surely come; therefore your miracle has no choice but to manifest!

For I am persuaded that neither death nor life, angels nor principalities, nor powers nor things present nor things to come, nor height nor depth, nor any other created thing shall be able to separate us from the love of God which is in Christ Jesus our Lord. (Romans 8:38-39)

CHAPTER 8:

I TOO HAVE TO LET GOD FINISH!

Being confident of this very thing, that He who has begun a good work in you will complete it until the day of Jesus Christ. (Philippians 1:6)

IF ANYONE HAS THOUGHT, PERHAPS IT IS EASY FOR SIOHVAUGHN to say you gotta let God finish, because she hasn't been through hardships like I have and doesn't understand how difficult even letting God finish is. But my friend, the truth is that I know hardships all too well, and have become acquainted with the process and pains of letting God finish. I know well the weight of waiting on the promise of God to manifest. I have danced with despair, entertained doubt, and confessed, "I give up!" and "I'm done!" I told God with pain in my heart, "The wait is becoming a weight!" I let God know with tear-filled eyes, "I'm sorry, but I can't wait anymore...it's too much."

It was during this season of my life that God gave me the revelation that we need to let Him finish, and the plan He had for me sharing it with you through this book. God desired to give this wisdom to me, and then through me, so that all of us will let Him finish what He began, and inherit all the promises and blessings He has in store for us!

God used the lives of many men and women throughout the Bible to reveal His heart and His ways to me so I wouldn't be burdened with despair and give up on God and what He promised. Then He began to minister to me about my own life, and had me look back over times when I let Him finish, and the rewards I received for doing so. I want to share just a few of these times with you and the wisdom God gave me to use while letting Him finish, knowing it will help transform and equip you to attain all that God has promised you!

My God Heals

There was a time in my life where I was so broken emotionally that I felt physical pain because of it. My stomach would hurt so terribly that I would ball up in the fetal position and lay in pain for hours at a time. The pain increased to a point whereby I could not breathe without it hurting. Everything was dark and I didn't see a way out. People I thought would be there for me were nowhere to be found and everyone who was willing to help me could not. I began to feel despair.

This is when God began to send people to tell me He had a plan for my life and that He would heal me. I had nothing except this Word from God. I learned that when you have a promise from God, you have everything you need. God is His word. The Bible says that if God is for you, who can be against you? Notice that you don't need anyone or anything else to be for you, but God! This is life-saving news for some reading this, because God is truly all they have. Well, God is telling you through me: If God is all you have; God is all you need! He is more than enough to help, heal, and restore you completely. I know this for a fact. During that time of darkness, I told God how my heart wasn't broken...perhaps that I could have handled. By my heart was shattered into pieces...so that it wasn't humanly possible to heal that. I needed God. And God willingly and joyfully healed me completely...just like He promised.

But it was a process of time before it happened. And some days the pain increased, and I thought maybe God forgot me, or maybe He changed His mind. God didn't change His mind, I just had to let God finish. Thankfully, I did just that and God did what He promised me, but above and beyond it. I am healed! My mind, emotions, heart, and soul have been healed from years of abuse from someone I loved deeply. God gave me beauty for those ashes, healed my heart, and even blessed me to love again! God did what He promised me and He is not a respecter of persons. What God did for me; He will do for you!

God Is a Restorer

It was God who taught me that there is a difference between being healed and being restored. Healing involved God mending the brokenness of my heart. The Lord restoring me involved God putting me back in a position where I had a do-over. For example, someone who goes through a devastating divorce and has their heart broken can be healed by God. They are no longer broken and their heart's mended. God's restoration for this person would be giving them another opportunity to be a wife and have a blessed marriage that doesn't end in divorce. As important as healing is, when God taught me this, I learned to pray for healing and restoration. I certainly needed both and the Lord promised me both. Now, I had experienced the healing God promised and all the pain I once felt was completely gone…to the point that what used to make me lose sleep and weight made me laugh. God had done it, but I longed to be restored.

Come to find out the longing was not my own. God longed to restore me and we had become one, and when you become one with someone, their desires become yours. I now had God's desires in my heart and the desire was strong. I wanted God to restore me as a woman of worth, because the abuse made me feel completely worthless. It is one thing to have low self-esteem, but I had no self-esteem. I believed the lies my abuser told me, and I stopped believing what God said about me. But God! He came to restore my worth, removing every lie the devil ever told me through the mouth of man and the media. God supplanted their lies with His everlasting truth. Oh, and now and forevermore, I am completely convinced that I am who God says I am, and I am worth what God says I am worth! I refuse to believe the lies of a Godless-man or God-forsaken media anymore. When it comes down to it, no one can speak on our worth, because it cannot be measured. My worth, and yours, is priceless! As far as God is concerned we are worth God dying for! That, my love, cannot be measured or purchased! Because God restored me, I now realize that I am fearfully and wonderfully made…and because God made me, and He doesn't make mistakes; I am not a mistake either. I have been conceived in love by Love Himself, and I have a purpose that's great, a destiny that's divine, and with God on my side I cannot lose. Beloved, our worth, as sons and daughters of God, is immeasurable, priceless, and unchanging! God gave it and nobody can take it away. God measured it and no man can fathom it!

God had restored me. I knew and believed the truth about my worth and because God always works from the inside out on us, He restored me on the inside first, by giving me a revelation of my worth and then, He began to restore my life outwardly. God promised me that He would realize the dreams I had put off in the past because I wanted to help my former spouse fulfill his. Jesus did it! I wanted to be a professional counselor and lawyer. God blessed me to graduate with my Bachelor's Degree in Psychology and obtain a Master's-Degree-level Certificate in Professional Counseling. The number of people God has blessed me to counsel is countless. God is faithful. God also just blessed me to graduate Magna Cum Laude from law school and open up a mediation firm, whereby I mediate and arbitrate legal cases for lawyers and judges. God then blessed me with a real estate investment company that God has used to restore lives by restoring their living. I had lost my home at one point, but God restored me with a house that to me is the most beautiful one so far that He has given me. Now, please understand that I am not tooting my horn; I am testifying about the goodness and faithfulness of God to restore. To my Father in heaven be all the glory! I tell you what I tell everyone else: Jesus did it! Jesus restored me inside and out. But what I have discussed with you is only the tip of the iceberg of what God has promised me. But as much as I want those promises to manifest in my life like yesterday, I see the good in waiting. It was in this waiting room that God gave me wisdom and revelation for my sake and yours, so you will not give up or faint while you wait… and instead inherit all of the promises God has for you. This is truly God's heart and desire for you, and it is mine, too. Beloved, one of the reasons God allowed me to experience waiting was to help you fulfill your destiny; and I am glad He did, because you are worth waiting for!

Rejoice the Rubbish is Gone!

Before we go, I felt God telling me to share with those of you who have experienced great hurt because your spouse or significant other left you for another partner, something that He explained to me. It really gave me perspective. God wants to heal you and give you His perspective too regarding the one who left with your partner. Some of you are experiencing bitterness towards the other woman, but it is time to be free and realize God has turned her, who was sent as a curse, into a blessing for you already. You can thank God for her, in fact. God explained this to me about the other woman or other man: They are like garbage collectors...a rubbish company! The one who left you is like the rubbish they collect. None of us get angry at, or resent, the garbage collector who comes once a week to take away all the trash we have. Instead, we thank God for him or her, because we realize trash is not something you keep in your life or home; you cast it out. Otherwise it can cause all sorts of problems, including but not limited to, bad smells making living there unbearable, bug infestation, and even sickness because of the toxic environment it creates. Thus, the garbage collector who comes and removes rubbish from your life is a blessing and someone we should be thankful for. Likewise, and greater, is the one who comes and collects the emotional garbage from our lives. This is exactly what strange men and women do. They remove what is toxic from your life. Thank God for them! Now that the garbage has been collected, God has room to restore you with a man or woman after God's own heart. Beloved, it's restoration time...so rejoice and renounce all bitterness. Your latter will be greater than your former! (Haggai 2:9).

Waiting-Room Wisdom

God is good, and a lot of what He has promised me He has given me already. There are, however, things I am waiting for God to finish. Thus, I too have to let God finish. While I have waited, God has given me what I call "Waiting-Room Wisdom." God is giving you this wisdom too, so that the wait doesn't become a weight to you, like it did me.

Before we get right into it, I want to share with you a revelation God gave me about why we wait. But first, let us agree that God loves us and does what is best for us…even if we don't understand it. Parents and caregivers, you will understand this probably more easily. When raising a child, there are things that a child may deeply desire, but you as a parent knowing them and all of what their desire entails, know that they are not ready for it. An untimely blessing can become a curse. This is why some people who leave an inheritance via a will to their children release portions of the inheritance at certain times in the child's life…the time when they can handle the blessing. And if parents being evil can give this good gift to their children of protection, even from blessings out of time, how much greater will God give good gifts to us, His children? Beloved, settle it in your heart and mind; God doesn't want to withhold anything good from you, but it is His job as your Father to know what is best for you and act accordingly. Let's trust His heart of love and accept the fact that sometimes we aren't ready just yet for the next level He is taking us to. But don't worry, God will get you ready and take you to the next level.

Also, sometimes the reason we wait is not because we are not ready, but because our destinies are tied to others and they may not be ready. God is preparing your destiny partner, so that when you all sail off together into destiny waters, your ship won't sink. And your destiny partner is worth the wait, because nobody fulfills his or her destiny alone. Even Jesus had twelve disciples, and help carrying His cross (Mark 15:21). Now, if Jesus had help, believe that we will need it too. None of us were meant to go at this thing called life alone. The late Dr. King realized, our destinies are divinely tied together whether we like it or not. Now, with understanding of why we wait, we should be more happy, because happy is the man who has understanding.

Let's begin discussing the waiting-room wisdom with what we should not do. We should not go after the blessing, keeping watch over it, but rather we should go after God and let Him make the blessings come after us. God used a natural illustration to show me why this is so important, and how when people don't do it the wait becomes a weight. The Lord showed me that praying to Him is bringing a care or concern to Him for help. This is like when someone brings someone they love to a doctor because they need help. Specifically, the Lord used a surgeon as an example. God showed me how when loved ones bring their family member to a surgeon because they need help, they have done the right thing. They can only help that family member so much, and so because they love them, they turn them over to someone who is well able to help them. However, once that loved one comes into the care of the surgeon, the family members aren't allowed in the surgery room…they are instructed to go into the waiting room. This is best for everyone. Having concerned loved ones in the surgery room could hurt the patient and leave them in a worse state than the one they were in when they arrived. Also, surgery can get really messy. This isn't something a loved one should be watching. It is likely to freak them out. Likewise, when God is handling a family member, it isn't the best idea to watch over Him performing the surgery. We aren't trained healers and our lack of understanding can produce fear when we see the sight of a surgical procedure. First sight of blood and we panic, or someone's pulse decreases significantly during the procedure and we despair, when the truth is that the surgeon deliberately and for the patient's good just had them sedated which intentionally slows the heart rate down. What looks to us like a lot of ups and downs are normal for the surgeon. But because we don't fully understand the healing process, the normal process of what it entails can turn into a horrifying reason to give up. This is why God is telling us not to watch over His shoulder or watch over the promise He made while He works. That is His job. The Bible says that God watches over His Word to perform it we are supposed to have our eyes on Jesus. The Bible says, "Looking unto Jesus the author and **finisher** of our faith." Jesus is a finisher! We can trust that He will finish, so let's return to the waiting room and stop peeking in the surgical areas of this process for our sake and the sake of our promise.

God also told me that while He finishes, "Don't wait to celebrate!" He used the scripture in Isaiah 54 to teach me what to do while I let Him finish: "Sing O barren, you who have not borne! Break forth into singing, and cry aloud, you who have not labored with child!" (Isaiah 54:1). Rejoice by faith with God, because He will surely do what He promised you. Don't postpone your joy anymore…God will do it! Enjoy your life right now, in this moment, regardless of what needs to be fixed. Look at your life like a house. Just because the contractor isn't finished repairing the basement, doesn't mean you can't enjoy the rest of your house knowing that basement will come out better than it was before! Every day is a blessing and we cannot wait to celebrate because of the presence of a problem, because on this side of heaven, problems exist. If we wait for all the problems to be resolved to celebrate, we may be waiting forever on this side. Not because any problem will continue to persist, but because once it's resolved the same devil will likely try to bring another one. The absence or presence of problems cannot be the determining factor of whether we are going to celebrate God and life. Even though the problem may still be trying to linger around, we can rejoice right now and celebrate who God is, what He has done, and the fact that He will do everything else He promised. This isn't for God's sake; it is for ours. The joy of the Lord is our strength (Nehemiah 8:10). The enemy knows this. So he tries to keep us from rejoicing and celebrating Jesus, because doing so gives us strength, and when you are strong, the wait doesn't feel like a weight to you. And even if you do feel a weight, you are strong enough to bear it.

Now that we know what not to do while we let God finish, let's look at what God said we should do. God said, "Enlarge the place of your tent, and let them stretch out the curtains of your dwellings; do not spare; lengthen your cords and strengthen your stakes. For you shall expand to the right and to the left, and your descendants will inherit the nations and make the desolate cities inhabited" (Isaiah. 54:2-3). In other words, prepare for the promises God made you. If you have faith in God, you will be ready. Waiting time is not idle time. This is a time where we rejoice and prepare. The Lord told me one day that true faith in God will have you ready for what He promised you. Ask God for wisdom to prepare for your promise…because the Lord will surely fulfill it! God always answers our prayers—in fact, He over-answers us!

Dare to Enlarge Your Prayer!

Everything that I have prayed and asked God for, He has done, or is currently doing. God is not a respecter of persons. Thus, God will answer your prayers, too. Not only does God answer prayers, He exceeds our expectations. And in doing so He has not failed me yet, and He won't fail **anyone** who trusts in Him and prays. God wants you to know this truth and experience the blessing of doing so. But before we can pray bold prayers, we have to know we are someone God will answer at all. We need to know that God will answer us if we call on Him. We see this truth throughout the Bible, but Jesus said it best, "For **everyone** who asks, receives, and **everyone** who seeks, finds, and to **everyone** who knocks, the door will be opened" (Matthew 7:8, Emphasis Mine). God tells us three times that **everyone** can receive from Him. If you are someone, then you a part of the "everyone" the Lord is talking about. God believed it so important for us to know and believe this truth, that He repeated Himself three times. Contrary to religious beliefs this includes sinners and saints.

Not only did He say it, but also we see God in action performing this very promise in the Word. The Bible says that "people throughout the village brought sick family members to Jesus and no matter what their diseases were, the touch of His hand healed **everyone**" (Luke 4:40). There it is; God healed everyone. Certainly, that multitude of people included sinners and saints. Nevertheless, Jesus healed them all. And Jesus is the same yesterday, today, and forevermore. That means if Jesus was willing then to help us all, He is willing now.

Furthermore, the Bible says, "He [God] makes His sun rise on the evil and on the good, and sends rain on the just and on the unjust" (Matthew 5:45, emphasis mine). Again, we see that God has blessed us all. It is vital that we understand and believe this truth, because again it is very contrary to religious beliefs. Religion tells people that God is harsh and unforgiving towards people, but when God speaks for Himself, and demonstrates His heart through His actions, we see that God is love and He delights in forgiving us all. "For God so loved **the world** that He gave His only begotten Son, that whosoever believes in Him shall not perish but have everlasting life. He did not send His Son into the world to condemn **the world**, but that through Him **the world** might be saved (John 3:16-17 Emphasis Mine). God's love for every one of us is why He sent Jesus to die! And in fact, Jesus died for all of our sins and God calls it just when He forgives us. The Bible says, "if we confess [say the same thing as God does] our sins, He is faithful and just to forgive us our sins and to cleanse us from all unrighteousness" (1 John 1:9, emphasis mine). You see; God considers it just to forgive us, because Jesus has died for all our sins and justified us. God says in Isaiah, "Let the wicked forsake his way, and the unrighteous man his thoughts; let him return to the Lord, and **He will have mercy** on him and to our God for **He will abundantly pardon**" (Isaiah 55:7). God has made it clear that He will have mercy and He will forgive…abundantly! That's the heart of our Father. It is good we know this truth about God's heart for us so we can do what God said and come to His throne boldly to get His help (Hebrews

4:16). Now, knowing this truth, every one of us reading this, regardless of our past or present standing with God, should pray big, bold prayers knowing God will answer us exceedingly, abundantly above all we can think or imagine.

I know from personal experience, that God answers prayers exceedingly. I remember when I had my first son, I was young, and the responsibilities were high, while my funds were low. I wanted us as a family to have a place of our own to live together in, and so I prayed. I prayed that God would allow us to get on the waiting list for free public housing. In other words, I prayed that we would live in the projects. God didn't answer that prayer; He over-answered my prayer, and instead of the projects He gave me penthouse living. What would He have done had I prayed for the penthouse? Therefore, beloved; dare to enlarge your prayers, because our loving Father always exceeds our expectations!

In Closing

Well, we see when it comes to needing to let God finish; I am no exception to the rule. I too have had to let God finish. And in doing so, I have learned that God and His promises are well worth the wait. Beloved, if you are waiting on God to do something, don't despair or give up. God is faithful to do all that He promised you, and will surprise you with even more of His goodness than you asked for. He will exceed your expectations. So use the wisdom God has given you throughout this book, including that from my own life, and you will inherit the promises and possess your promised land, knowing that you are not alone in the process because we all at some point in our lives have to let God finish. And as you can see from my life and the lives of those herein, God always finishes what He begins, and He always fulfills His promises. And the transforming truths I've shared with you today are proof that God will make it worth your wait.

Therefore, beloved, rest knowing that God who promised you will faithfully watch over that Word of promise and He will perform it!

> Now to Him who is able to do exceedingly abundantly above all that we ask or think, according to the power that works in us, to Him be glory. (Ephesians 3:20)

CHAPTER 9:

IT IS FINISHED!

In beginning was the Word and the Word was
with God and the Word was God, and the Word
became flesh and dwelt among us. (John 1:1)

GOD CHOSE TO USE MANY PEOPLE'S LIVES IN ORDER TO GIVE US
a revelation of His love for us and His ways throughout this book. He
has done so in order that we won't give up on Him, or the promises
He made to us, while we wait for them to manifest. All of these people's lives are good examples, and I know we have all learned a lot,
but the greatest of these is the example of the life of God Himself as
He walked it out here on the earth as Jesus. Jesus is God (John 1:1).
Yes, that is right. God reduced Himself to human flesh and dwelt
among His people to save us, make us righteous, and provide us
with an inheritance so vast it cannot be measured. God is good! And
while it is true that God is Almighty God, El Shaddi, He was born as
a man. Thus, He became subject to all the temptations and sufferings
mankind faces while on this broken vessel called earth.

Yes, God Himself felt sadness and wept (John 11:35). He felt the pain of betrayal and the worst of rejections…even from His own family (John 7:5). God did this for many reasons. Four of which the Lord led me to share with you briefly are (1) He loves us; (2) He had to be born as a man so that He could die in order to save all of us who believe in Him (because as God, He cannot die); (3) Jesus developed a unique compassion for us that came through Him suffering as a Man, and as a result of that He sympathizes with us in ways we have yet to fully understand (Hebrews 4:15); and (4) He had to be born a Man pursuant to God's laws in order to redeem us from the curse.

This revelation is much deeper than what I can share right now, but perhaps God will expound through me even more in the near future. However, for now, it is important that we understand that Jesus is God-Man. He is absolutely God, but became an actual Man, and as an actual Man He fully understands all that we go through and the temptation of giving up and giving in—because Jesus, too, had to let God finish!

The Servant Is Not Greater Than the Master

Like us, God made Jesus many promises while He was here on the earth, and Jesus had to keep believing God would do what He promised, when faced with the most difficult challenges any man would ever face while on this earth. Without question, we as humans face various trials, which can be trying, but none of us will have to face all that Jesus did. God put upon Jesus, and He willing took it, all the sin, punishment therefrom, and all the curse of everyone who ever lived, and ever would live! Again, I am sure we have been through difficult challenges, but not like what Jesus suffered. All the evil weight of the whole world fell hard on Him, because He took our place on the cross and gave us His, that we might be saved. No wonder the Bible says, "God is love."

So we know that although Jesus is God, as a Man He suffered as a man, but to an extent that we won't ever have to, because He did it for us already. This doesn't mean that we won't have serious trials and tribulations. Jesus Himself said in the world you will have trouble, but be of good cheer, I have overcome the world (John 16:33). Thus we are not exempted from some trouble or attacks from the devil... not even Jesus escaped that fate while on this fallen earth. And if Jesus, the Creator, didn't escape trials, we as the creation ought to know that we will face trials, too. Jesus told us to remember, "A servant is not greater than his Master. If they persecuted Me, they will also persecute you. If they kept My Word, they will keep yours also" (John 15:20). In other words, if Jesus, the greater One, was subjected to difficulties and tribulation, that explains why we as His servants aren't exempted. The good news is that if we share in Jesus suffering, we share in His glory! (Romans 8:17). And when God glorifies you, you are glorified, highly exalted, and receive double honor! Everyone faces difficulties, believers and unbelievers, but the difference for the sons and daughters of God is that God has taken an oath promising us victory. Jesus Himself wrote our story, and its end, before the foundation of the world, and the outcome is we win. We win, because God has made us victorious and causes everything to work together for our good!

Let's take a closer look at just a few examples of sufferings Jesus was subjected to as a human. Some of you reading them may find them all too familiar. Jesus suffered a lot, from the time He was conceived. At the onset of His life, He was persecuted and hunted down because orders for His execution had been released by an evil king (Matthew 2:16). Then He was placed in a manger, a fancy word for a place where animals live and even use the bathroom! (Matthew 2:1). And that was just the beginning. The sufferings worsened. Jesus was, as the Bible says, "despised and rejected by men, a Man of sorrows and acquainted with grief. And we hid, as it were, our faces from Him. He was despised, and we did not esteem Him" (Isaiah 53:3).

Now the despising and rejection didn't just come from strangers, but from His biological family, too. The Bible says that Jesus' own brothers didn't believe in Him, and in His own hometown He could not do many miracles…I suppose he was just a carpenter to them, not the Messiah (Mark 6:4-5). Imagine the pain. I know that some of us don't have to imagine, we have had similar experiences with family rejection and the pain that comes from it. God knows this hurt is deep. I love what Jesus teaches us about family, because if we really believe this, the devil won't be able to wound us at all or at least not as deeply when blood relatives reject us. Jesus said, "My family is these doing the will of God" (Luke 8:21). That truth is liberating, because the enemy tries hard to wound us via biological relatives, but when you know your family extends well beyond your blood and the confines of your last name, you realize that you have more family for you than against you! By the way, I am doing the will of God, and if you are too, we are family!

As Jesus grew, the sufferings did, too. Don't get me wrong, it wasn't all bad. The Bible says that Jesus grew in wisdom and stature and even from a young age He was about His Father's business (Luke 2:52). But later on in life, Jesus was persecuted by the religious leaders of His time, and one of His very own disciples betrayed Him for money and set Him up to be captured by people who wanted to murder Him. But because He is God and Man, they couldn't arrest Him; Jesus had to surrender. Making it crystal clear that Jesus was not murdered, He laid down His life for us (John 10:18).

Then after being betrayed, He was falsely accused, falsely arrested, and then subjected to a corrupted trial and an unjust judge, who knew he was innocent but sentenced anyway to the cruelest flogging and scourging (John 19:1). And all of this might have been more bearable, except that at the time Jesus needed His friends the most, He found the fewest of them around. His dear friend Peter denied Him three times with cursing, and swearing He never knew Jesus (John 18). The Bible says Jesus was beaten so badly that He became unrecognizable. Then they placed a wooden cross on His shredded back, that was already pouring forth blood, and sentenced Him to death for a crime He never committed (Matthew 27:18). But He didn't die before they spat on Him, publically humiliated Him, even stripping Him completely naked in front of multitudes of people, including His own mother! (John 19:25).

Then came the ultimate suffering: He was separated from God! Wow! At least when we face trials, God is with us and for us. But for our sake, God forsook His own Son whom He loves deeply. He put Jesus to death so that we would escape it. God definitely loves us!

After all these sufferings and many I haven't mentioned, Jesus proclaimed the all-powerful word "Complete!" (In the language He spoke). Then He gave up His life…headed to hell and waged a war on the devil that left Satan utterly defeated. Jesus went through hell (literally), but God was faithful and caused His Son to overcome and gave Him everlasting victory, and as we will soon see, God also had a divine powerful purpose for all the pain Jesus endured.

Now Jesus, like us, had been given many promises from God… but faced all manners of evil that would tempt Him to give up on God and every promise He made Him while He waited on God to manifest them. Jesus too had to trust God enough to let God finish! And if Jesus had to do this, we most certainly do too. Remember, "The servant is not greater than the Master." Jesus knows what it is like for God to make a promise and the opposite seems to occur, and He knows that we need faith and trust in God all the more at times like this. By way of example, God promised Jesus He would be a King forever, but Jesus was a carpenter, often disrespected by His own family…and the only crown He ever wore was made of thorns crushing His skull. The only royal apparel He received was placed mockingly on this bleeding back by His enemies as they spit in His face and flogged Him until He was unrecognizable (Mark 15:17, Isaiah 53:5). Wow, some kingship. Come on, I know some of you are thinking it. I did. This isn't looking at all like what God promised

Him. In fact it is an extreme opposite. Much less has caused some to completely despair, but Jesus didn't give up on His Father, knowing that God is faithful and He will do all He promised. It is written, "He who calls you is faithful, who also will do it" (1 Thessalonians 5:24).

Another example of Jesus having to trust God and let Him finish came from the promise "that at the name of Jesus every knee should bow, of those in heaven, and of those under, and that every tongue would confess that Jesus Christ is Lord, to the glory of God the Father" (Philippians 2:10-11). However, the only knees that seemed to be bowed were Jesus' knees as He fell under the weight of the curse of that cross as He hauled it on His bleeding back as people laughed, mocked, and treated Him as if He deserved the hell He was going through. Needless to say, as a Man Jesus, too, had to let God finish!

There was another trying time in Jesus' life when He could have given up on God. It was right after a time when God announced to Jesus, "This is My beloved Son in whom I am well pleased" (Matthew 3:17). Right after God told Jesus these endearing words of affirmation, the Bible says, "Immediately the Spirit drove Jesus into the wilderness. And He was there in the wilderness forty days, [tested] by Satan, and was with the wild beast; and the angels ministered to Him (Mark 1:12-13). This would have caused some of us to fall out with God, because the human reaction to being told by God, "You are my beloved Son in whom I am well pleased" and then thereafter being immediately driven by God's Spirit, not the devil, into the wilderness to be tested would have been great disappointment with God! But any animosity against God would have come from a lack of understanding, not unfaithfulness from God. God is good, whether we are in or out of the wilderness…and He is with us and for us at all times in all places working everything together for our good.

Jesus believed this and knew God loved Him and so He held on to the words of His Father calling Him His beloved and telling Him He is well pleased with Him...even while in the wilderness. The wilderness is a lonely, dry place where nothing grows outside of a miracle from God. Yet Jesus believed God. His faith saved Him. Jesus said this to others many times...but His faith in God's love for Him and goodness saved Him. This is why God told us, "Provision always precedes the problem." God knew what was about to happen to His Son; therefore God prepared Jesus beforehand with His word of affirmation, so that He would not only survive in the wilderness, but thrive there. The love God showed Jesus, affirming Him, and the very power of God's spoken Word sustained Jesus in that wilderness, causing Him to come out victorious and fulfill His destiny...saving the entire world from their own sins. This is why God tells us that in all of our getting, we are to get understanding. Because happy is the man who has understanding (Proverbs 4:7). That is surely the case, because when God gave me this understanding, I got happy! Now, granted; all the time we don't have understanding prior to facing a challenge, and when this happens God has simply, but powerfully, led me to this instruction, "When you can't understand My hand, trust My heart."

I felt from God it was important that we take a moment to meditate on the truths contained in this section, because we often think of Jesus in the fullness of His being God, and fail to recall Him as a Man, who is familiar with everything we go through as human beings. Jesus can relate, contrary to popular, misguided belief. Jesus knows everything you are going through, not because He is all knowing, although this is true, but because He lived in human flesh (Romans 8:3). He knows what you are going through because He went through it. Now, when we mediate on this truth, we more easily talk to Jesus and know that He doesn't judge us in our weaknesses because He understands it! I'm glad He came in human flesh because he does understand what we endure; and the even better news is that

Jesus is also God. This means that Jesus is more than a shoulder to cry on, He is the One who is powerful enough to take everything in your life and work it together for your good! Jesus being God and being Man is perfect for us. He sympathizes with us as a Man, and as God speaks one Word and changes our entire life for the better!

What Jesus Did While Letting God Finish

We can see from just the examples above that Jesus had to let God finish, too. At this point, most if not everyone reading this can agree, we all need to let God finish. But that revelation begs this important question: "What do we do, while we let God finish?" Now, although God used my life to give direction in this area, there is nothing like looking directly at the Messiah, who we can without any doubt, draw wisdom, from.

So let's look at what Jesus did while He let God finish the work that God began in His life, so that we too, like Jesus, can run this race called life, fulfill our destiny, and receive everything God promised us!

The Bible says, "looking unto Jesus, the author and finisher of our faith, who **for the joy that was set before Him** endured the cross, despising the shame, and has sat down at the right hand of the throne of God" (Hebrews 12:2). We see from this Bible verse that Jesus set His face like flint on what God promised Him, while letting God finish. He looked expectantly for what God promised Him and let that be His focus. If Jesus, the Master, had to focus on the promise, instead of the problem, in order to endure life's trials; we the servants had better do the same. This means that if we are going through a trying time, we must focus on what God promised us, not the problem. The promises of God a lot of times are what make enduring the problem plausible. It gives us hope...something good to look forward to while we go through the trials of life. King David put it this way: "I would have lost heart, unless I had believed that I would see the goodness of the Lord in the land of the living" (Psalm 27:13). In other words, David believed and meditated on the promises, and the goodness of God, because he knew that if he didn't, he would surely give up hope. This wise instruction he gave us is one we should follow...especially since Jesus Himself used this same wisdom. Therefore, let us focus on God's miracle and not the seemingly insurmountable mountain we are facing. For God has promised us, even concerning the mountain (representing serious opposition), "if you have faith as a mustard seed, you will say to this mountain, 'Move from here to there,' and it will move; and nothing will be impossible for you" (Matthew 17:20). And since God has given each one of us a measure of faith, we know we have enough faith to say to any mountain be removed...and it has to go! This is a promise from God and one of the many promises you can focus on while you let God finish, and like Jesus, see every promise come to pass!

Another important thing Jesus did while letting God finish was to entrust His family to God and not allow them to take Him off the course God set Him on. One day, during Jesus' youth, He and His parents went to Jerusalem to celebrate the Passover (Luke 2:41). When His parents left Jerusalem they didn't realize Jesus wasn't with them or among their relatives and friends who traveled with them, so they turned around and went back to Jerusalem to find Him. When they did, Jesus was in the midst of teachers inside the synagogue, asking questions and listening to them teach (Luke 2:46). Jesus' parents were pretty upset and anxious about His lingering behind in Jerusalem. What was Jesus response? "Did you not know that I must be about My Father's business?" (Luke 2:49). Jesus, even as a young 12-year-old, was focused on His Father's business and didn't let family detour Him. In order to do this, Jesus had to trust God completely with His family. We must do the same. We must know that God loves our family more than we do, and it was God's love that caused Him to send Jesus to die for them. God is love. A pure, unconditional, everlasting love that will take care of our family and us.

On another occasion, when Jesus had already officially begun His ministry here on the earth, He was teaching a multitude of people about God. His "biological" brothers and His mother came and were calling Him. When someone from the crowd told Jesus that they were seeking Him, He responded, while looking into the crowd, "Here are My mother and My brothers! For whoever does the will of God is My brother and My sister and mother" (Mark 3:35). This may seem strong, but this strength is necessary to do the will of God. The enemy will try to use anything he knows you care about, including family to try and distract you. Therefore, to fulfill our destiny, we have to entrust our family to God and not allow hell to distract us through them. God is trustworthy. Furthermore, Jesus promised, "Assuredly, I say to you, there is no one who has left house or brothers or sisters or father or mother or wife or children or lands, for My sake and the gospel's, who shall not receive a hundredfold now in this time…and in the age to come, eternal life" (Mark 10:29). Beloved, with a promise like this, from a faithful God like Jesus, we can trust God with everything—including our family.

Lastly, but certainly not exhaustive, is another one of the things that Jesus did while letting God finish. Namely, Jesus refused to be distracted in general! Beloved, this is crucial. I know sometimes, especially in charismatic churches, we are taught that a sign of the devil coming against your life is when all hell seems to break loose in your life. This can be true; however, the devil doesn't always come into our lives screaming, shouting, and knocking things over. Often he comes into our lives very subtly via distractions. And because he is evil, he doesn't use little distractions that would just irritate someone. No, he gives it his defeated all and uses serious things like matters of life and death and/or family matters.

We see this in the life of Jesus. The devil put it in the heart of the Jewish leaders of that day to kill Jesus. I must admit, being hunted down like prey, for the purpose of being killed, is a pretty powerful distraction…after all it is a matter of life and death. I am so glad that God used this distraction in the life of Jesus to teach us, because we can all likely agree that matters of life and death are the most serious matters. However, even with the most serious circumstance, we still see that Jesus set His face like flint, stayed focused on doing God's will, and refused to be distracted. One of the examples of this is found in the book of Luke, which occurred right after Jesus finished reading the scroll from Isaiah in the synagogue. Jesus had just announced to the people that He was God. The Jews rejected him and the idea that He was God in the flesh (Luke 4:18-30). In fact, they were filled with rage, and rose up to try and push Jesus off of a cliff so they could kill Him. What did Jesus do? He didn't go into hiding. Nor did He go into prayer asking God questions He already knew the answer to, such as, "Are you sure You called Me?" Instead, Jesus went into another city, taught the Word of God, and cast a demon out of someone in need (Luke 4:31-37). Jesus refused to be fearful and distracted by the devil even while facing the threat of being murdered.

And in case anyone is thinking it's not possible for them to remain undistracted when it comes to matters of life and death, and that only Jesus could be facing the threat of murder and keep doing the will of God undistracted; God wants to show you it is possible for you and others to accomplish this with the Lord's help…which you have. God would not tell us to do anything without first giving us the power to do it.

Nehemiah is a perfect example of this occurring. Nehemiah's purpose from God was to rebuild the city and the gates of his people in Jerusalem, which had been burned down. Well needless to say, as soon as the enemy found out Nehemiah and the others God sent were rebuilding, the distractions began. First came the mocking and public humiliation. Some enemies of the builders, Sanballot and Tabiah, mocked them and told them their work would never amount to anything...and they did so publically in an effort to humiliate them, hoping shame would cause them to go into hiding. Had that distraction prevailed, the builders would have certainly ceased from their work and the walls would have gone unfinished. It isn't easy to do the will of God on a public platform, while being publically humiliated (trust me, I know). But Nehemiah, prayed to God to deal with his enemies, and kept on building, and substantial progress was made! (Nehemiah 4:4-5).

When the enemy saw that this first distraction didn't work, he took his distractions up a notch. Namely, Tabiah and Sanballot gathered together with others to conspire and plot the death of Nehemiah and the other builders, while using their words to try to put them in fear so that they couldn't build (Nehemiah 4:7). This is an old tactic of the devil...the use of fear to distract the people of God from their purpose, the reason being is that fear can be paralyzing. But I love Nehemiah's response. He told the people, "Do not be afraid of them. Remember the Lord, great and awesome" (Nehemiah 4:14).

The builders kept building. Notably, after this failing attempt of the enemy, he became more desperate and crafty. Having failed at distracting Nehemiah as his enemy, he pretended to be his friend so that he could kill him. Needless, to say that distraction failed as well. The builders remained focused on what God sent them to do and refused to be distracted by hell even while facing the threat of death! The result? The wall was rebuilt, God was glorified, and the builders fulfilled their divine purpose in life...proving once again that the devil is a trying failure! Therefore, like Jesus and Nehemiah, let us set our face like flint undistracted by that defeated foe and allow God to finish through us what He began!

No More Distractions!

It is vital that we take a moment and look more deeply into this. You see, the enemy has no power at all to destroy your destiny; therefore, he tries to delay it. The number one method of trying to accomplish this is via distractions. Now keep in mind that God Himself calls the devil cunning and crafty. In other words, the enemy is shrewd, and operates in an evil wisdom. Thus, when the enemy tries to distract us, he doesn't do it in a way whereby his evil agenda would be obvious, and he doesn't use unimportant things or people to attempt to distract…he is too crafty for that. Instead, he subtly uses things, or people, who he thinks are of the utmost importance in our lives to distract us…and it's usually those things or people he thinks we will worry over, and be full of cares about. This is why Jesus urged us, even regarding important matters, "Do not worry" and "Take My yoke upon you…My yoke is easy and My burden is light" (Matthew 11:30). Again, in another place the scriptures say, "Cast your *cares* on Him (Jesus) for He cares for you." Notice that Jesus tells us to cast our cares (those things we care about) on Him and take His yoke, which is easy and light. The things we care about tend to be the things that weigh heavy on our hearts when trouble comes. Therefore, the lesson is this: no matter how important the subject matter, or person, the enemy uses to try to distract us, we must take heed to Jesus' wisdom and not worry, but rather cast the care on Him. Because when we don't worry, we don't get distracted. And when we don't get distracted, we fulfill our destiny and realize that the weapon the devil formed couldn't prosper anyway! For it is written, "No weapon formed against you shall prosper" (Isaiah 54:17).

The devil also tries to distract us (those who have a heart for God) with religion. The devil did this to Martha, the sister of Mary and Lazarus whom Jesus raised from the dead. And because this serpent is crafty, he didn't use just anything to distract Martha; he used her desire to serve Jesus. That's a dirty trick, but he is a dirty devil. Now, there isn't anything wrong with serving Jesus, but when Jesus has called you to serve Him, and is leading you in that service, the yoke upon you in doing so is easy, and the burden is light. That doesn't mean there will be no challenges or opposition, but you will see that even in the midst of the challenges, you have a peace that surpasses all understanding (Philippians 4:7). The Lord pointed this out to me because He wants us to know and understand that the enemy will even use what appears as "serving God" to distract people from fulfilling their destiny or doing what God actually has called them to do in that season of their life. Martha should have been doing what her sister Mary was doing, and that is sitting at the feet of Jesus and allowing Him to serve her by filling her with His Word. Jesus Himself said, "the Son of Man didn't come to be served but to serve" (Mark 10:45). And when you think about it, yes it is humbling, but it also makes perfect sense. Jesus is God! Does God need us, or do we need God? We need God, of course…after all He is God, and we are human beings. We cannot give anything that is worth something unless we first allow God to give it to us. For apart from Him we can do nothing.

Martha tried to give out to Jesus, while running on empty and ended up worried, distracted, and troubled about *many* things! Not one or two things…but many things. This is why it is important that we take heed to what Jesus said and do the one thing that is needful. Jesus intentionally said "needful." I'm so glad because we know that the enemy tries to use needs to distract people. I'm sure the devil made Martha think she needed to serve Jesus. But Jesus, who cannot lie and loves us deeply, said only one thing is needful and that is us allowing Jesus to feed us and serve us. We would be wise to take Him at His Word and just believe Him. Realizing this and taking our rightful place in our relationship with God, Him as the Father and we as the children, is true humility. Trying to be our own God is pride, and trying to be a god to the only One who actually is God is crazy pride! My prayer is that we won't walk in pride because God resists the proud, but He gives grace to the humble. I make this prayer because God taught me pride comes in many forms. God let me know when someone is full of worry and care, pride is present; and when pride is present God is resisting; and if God, the only One who can meet the need and resolve the problem that they are worried about, is resisting the proud, the need is going unmet and the problem is persisting. This vicious cycle has to end. We must humble ourselves and recognize that without God we can do nothing and He alone is our provider and problem solver. The sooner we do this, the sooner worries, cares, and distractions fade away and the sooner our needs are met and problems are resolved in our favor. Remember, Martha, was "distracted with serving" and worried and troubled about many things. One of those things was serving God (Luke 10:40). Yet Jesus told her, what He is telling us today, even when it comes to serving Him: "one thing is needful" (Luke 10:42). That one thing is getting at Jesus' feet and allowing Him to feed us His Word. My prayer for my own life and yours is that we will be like Mary, and chose the good part that won't be taken from us, renouncing all distractions, especially those from religious spirits.

Before we close this section, I wanted to share with you a very interesting thing revealed to me, which Jesus didn't allow to distract Him from fulfilling His divine purpose either. It was the blessings of God that He watched manifest. Jesus, respectfully and gratefully, didn't linger and marvel too long in the miracles He performed, but rather He kept it moving. For example—and there are tons of them—Jesus healed a woman who had had a bleeding condition for 12 years. He stopped to minister to the woman, but not to marvel at the miracle. He went straight from healing her to raise Jarius' daughter from the dead! (Mark 5). This isn't a sign of ungratefulness or evil familiarity with God; it is a sign of true faith. Because when you know that God is able and willing, you aren't in shock, or stuck like a deer in headlights, marveling over the miracle. We as believers should be seeing miracles, signs, and wonders every day. This is our rule, not our exception. Jesus said, miracles, signs, and wonders will follow those who believe (Mark 16:17). Again, for the believer who believes God is willing and able, miracles, signs, and wonders should be commonplace! That is not a sign of ungratefulness; it is proof of real faith in God. So let us be grateful like Jesus, without becoming drunk with the wine of God's well doing, and remain undistracted even by blessings.

The Purpose of His Pain

God loves Jesus, and He did not allow Him to suffer like He did without good reasons. Namely, God allowed this for us, because He loves us deeply, and Jesus acquiesced to the sufferings because He loves us very deeply too. Yes, all the sufferings were for our sake and benefit. The Bible says, "Therefore, in all things He had to be made like His brethren, that He might be a merciful and faithful High Priest in things pertaining to God, to make propitiation for the sins of the people" (Hebrews 2:17). We can see from this verse that one of the reasons for Jesus' suffering was to develop mercy in Him toward us as human beings. God mentions Jesus being made like His brethren (us) so that He might be merciful and a faithful High Priest. In order to be a High Priest, you had to be human. God allowed Jesus to be born a human being, and allowed Him to endure the troubles we face on this earth that He might be merciful toward us and faithful as our High Priest.

This is a great gift from God. God has promised us that Jesus, as our High Priest, is faithful. As our High Priest, Jesus represents us before God, and as long as Jesus is acceptable to God we are, too. It is written as the High Priest goes, so goes Israel (the children of God).

Jesus is God's beloved, in whom He is well pleased, and because Jesus is our High Priest; we are also forever God's beloved in whom He is well pleased! Not only that but our High Priest is merciful and not judgmental to our shortcomings! And that blessing was birthed out of pain. Now, I don't thank God that Jesus was in pain, but I surely thank Him for the purpose of the pain.

God also had divine purpose in the pain He allowed Jesus to suffer on and prior to the cross. The Bible says in Isaiah, "But [in fact] He has borne our grief, and carried our sorrow and pains; yet we [ignorantly] assumed that He was stricken, struck down by God and degraded and humiliated [by Him]. But He was wounded for our transgressions, He was crushed for our wickedness [our sin, our injustice, our wrongdoing]; The punishment [required] for our well-being *fell* on Him, and by His strips (wounds) we are healed" (Isaiah 53:4-5). God didn't allow Jesus to suffer because of anything He did wrong. Jesus suffered in our place. All this punishment was for us, but Jesus traded places with us, taking on our sins, including all the punishment and curse for them, and died a death due an evil sinner, and then went to hell… all of which we deserved. He then gave us His place as God's beloved in whom He is well pleased, and made us children of God and heirs of God. Jesus saved us from all our sins and the consequences of them…including hell. He also justified us in His own blood, making us rightful heirs to all of God's blessings. And if that wasn't enough, God allowed for Jesus to be beaten beyond recognition, stripped naked in front of a garrison of soldiers, had a crown made of thorns crushed into His skull and His skin ripped to pieces in our place, in order to heal us from every sickness and disease and bear for us both sorrow, pain and shame! Believers, we are healed. What Jesus suffered for our wholeness and health is sufficient. Don't accept, or believe, anything less than what God promised: by His strips we are healed! (Isaiah 53:5). Thank God for not giving us what we deserved, but rather giving us His grace instead. And if God did all of this when we were His enemies, what won't He do for us now that we are His sons and daughters? I declare to you this truth: God won't withhold anything good from us! Again, I don't rejoice in the fact that Jesus had to suffer, but I do rejoice in the purpose God had for that pain!

God changes not. If God had a purpose for Jesus' pain, He has it for any pain you have suffered too. I believe to a large extent that the purpose is the same as Jesus' pain suffered...to develop mercy and empathy. I know that I went about my own life, not intentionally, but definitely erroneously, not thinking or caring much for anyone but my own self and my immediate family. After God allowed the pain others caused me to enter my life, I remember taking time to think about other people and what they may be going through. I would take long walks through multimillion-dollar neighborhoods and pray, asking God to have mercy on those who lived in those big houses. By then my own sufferings had been instrumental in teaching me that being rich doesn't make you happy; in fact it has often caused people pain they otherwise would have never known. Note that riches are not the problem. The Bible says, the blessings of the Lord makes one rich and He adds no sorrow with it (Proverbs 10:22). And every gift from God is good and perfect (James 1:17). Therefore riches are not the problem; they are a gift from God. The problem is that there is a tendency for some rich people to depart from God, because they don't think they need Him once that they have their false god, money. And it is very hard to tell them anything (Proverbs 28:11). They often disdain wise counsel. This is extremely deceiving. Jesus Himself said it is easier for a camel to go through the eye of a needle than for a rich man to enter the Kingdom of God (Matthew 19:24). However, all hope isn't lost. Jesus also said, with God all things are possible, including being rich and still loving and following God. Now, those of you who know me; you see me as merciful and compassionate, but it wasn't until I suffered that this transformation took place in me. God has used me to help so many people, and I understand and see now that God had a divine purpose in the pain He permitted me to suffer. And as painful as it was, I thank my Heavenly Father for His purpose. It is with God by my side and this compassion He developed in me through a painful time, that I am able to co-labor with Christ, fulfill my destiny and impact this world for the better. Beloved, if you have endured pain, God has a purpose for allowing it and it is good. He is working everything, including that pain, together for your good!

It is Finished

Who knew that injustice, sorrow, and pain would be the road that leads to salvation, health, and righteousness? God knew. He knows everything and He loves us more than we may ever truly understand. Therefore we can trust God. Jesus did. In fact He needed too. Surely, it did not look like the way God took Jesus—the shameful cursed cross—was the way to glory and the eternal exaltation God promised Him, but it was. Jesus had to trust God when He said the works were finished before the foundations of the world. Not only that, but Jesus had to not give up while God finish manifesting on earth what was already finished in heaven for His life. Beloved, we, like Jesus, must let God finish, knowing that as children of the God who goes before us, it actually is already finished!

I make known the end from the beginning, from ancient times, what is still to come. I say, 'My purpose will stand, and I will do all that I please.' (Isaiah 46:10 NIV)

CLOSING WORDS

He who calls you is faithful, who also will
do it. (1 Thessalonians 5:14).

In the Bible God reveals His heart toward us, which is
filled with love and rich with mercy for us. He reveals His hand, which
is filled with power and complete in provision. And He reveals to us
His ways, which are perfect, proven and trust worthy. In this book,
God has expounded on these truths, proving to us that all we have to
do, regardless of any opposition, in order to receive all God has for
us is to let God finish! And having gained a deeper understanding
of what Jesus did for us on the cross, we know that everything concerning us, the children of God, is finished! God has proven this to
us through the lives of every man and woman He used in this book,
including Jesus. Beloved, we can enter into rest. The work is finished.
God is for us and He will fulfill His promises to us. Therefore, like the
men and women of God herein; let God finish, and you too will see
the manifested glory and faithfulness of our loving Heavenly Father!
It is Finished! (John 19:30)

NOTES

1. Nelson NKJV Study Bible Barl D. Radmacher, Th.D; Ronald B. Allen; H Wayne House 1997

2. Thayer's Greek-English Lexicon of the New Testament Joseph H. Thayer 2015

3. Https://www.biblegateway.com (June 23, 2018 at 6:00 pm EST).

4. www.biblehub.com (NLT). July 2, 2018 at 6:22 pm CST).

5. "Letter from Birmingham Jail," Dr. Martin Luther King Jr., April 16, 1963, http://kinginstitute.standford.edu/king-papers/documents/letter-birmingham-jail

PRAYER OF SALVATION

If there is anyone who wants to inherit all of God's great promises, starting with salvation and complete forgiveness of all their sins, please pray the following prayer with me: Lord Jesus I receive the fullness of your love and believe you were crucified for all my sins and rose from the dead for my justification. I receive you as my Lord and Savior, and I receive every promise you made for me, and my whole house in Jesus name I pray!

A SPECIAL THANK YOU

A very special thank you to all the men and women who reached out to me in order to share with me how my first book, The True Story for God's Glory: The Life of Siohvaughn L. Funches-Wade, blessed and transformed their lives. I pray God does even greater works for you through this new masterpiece He wrote through me.

LET US HEAR FROM YOU

If this book has impacted and blessed your life, I would love to hear from you. You can share the good news with me at: www.awow-woman.com

ALSO WRITTEN BY THE AUTHOR

THE TRUE STORY FOR GOD'S GLORY:
THE LIFE OF SIOHVAUGHN L. FUNCHES-WADE

STAY CONNECTED WITH THE AUTHOR
Stay connected with Siohvaughn Funches through the following:
www.awowwoman.com
info@awowwoman.com
Facebook.com
Instagram.com
Twitter.com